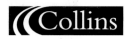

What Shall I Paint?

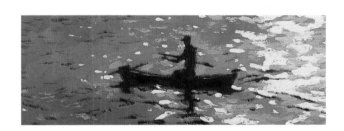

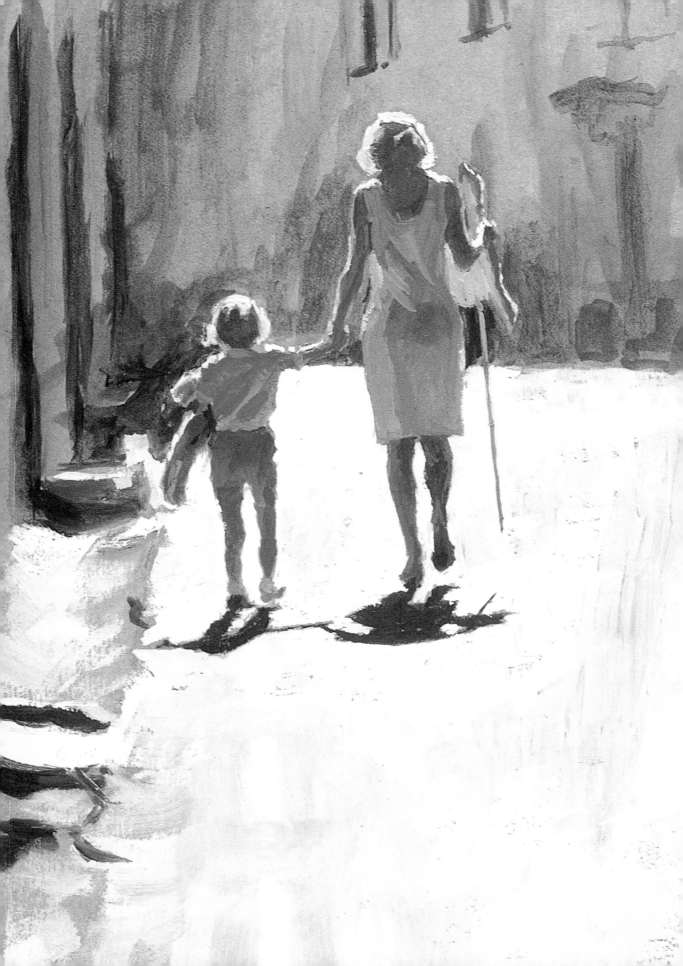

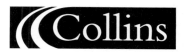

What Shall I Paint?

Finding the right subject in watercolour, oil and acrylic

HAZEL SOAN

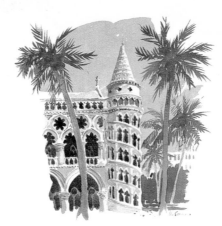

To John and Sean, for their company and love

First published in 2001 by
Collins, an imprint of
HarperCollins*Publishers*
77-85 Fulham Palace Road
Hammersmith, London W6 8JB

This edition first published in paperback in 2003

The Collins website address is:
www.collins.co.uk

© Hazel Soan, 2001

A catalogue record for this book is available from the British Library.

Editor: Geraldine Christy
Layout Designer: Julie Francis
Photographer: Laura Knox

ISBN 0 00 715617 0

Colour reproduction by Colourscan, Singapore
Printed and bound by Rotolito Lombarda, Italy

ACKNOWLEDGEMENTS

The author and publishers are grateful to the following source for artists' quotations throughout the book: *Artists on Art* (pub. John Murray, 1976). The quotation on page 59 is taken from THE *Philosophy of Andy Warhol (From A to B and Back Again)* (pub. Harcourt Brace, 1975). The painting on page 71 is reproduced courtesy of Rosenstiel's; and those on pages 46, 49 and 106 are reproduced courtesy of London Contemporary Art.

PAGE 1: **Lake of Stars,** *12 x 36 cm (4½ x 14 in), oil on board*
PAGE 2: **La Baguette,** *26.5 x 19 cm (10½ x 7½ in), oil on board*
PAGE 4: **Indian Dreams,** *20 x 13 cm (8 x 5 in), watercolour on paper*

CONTENTS

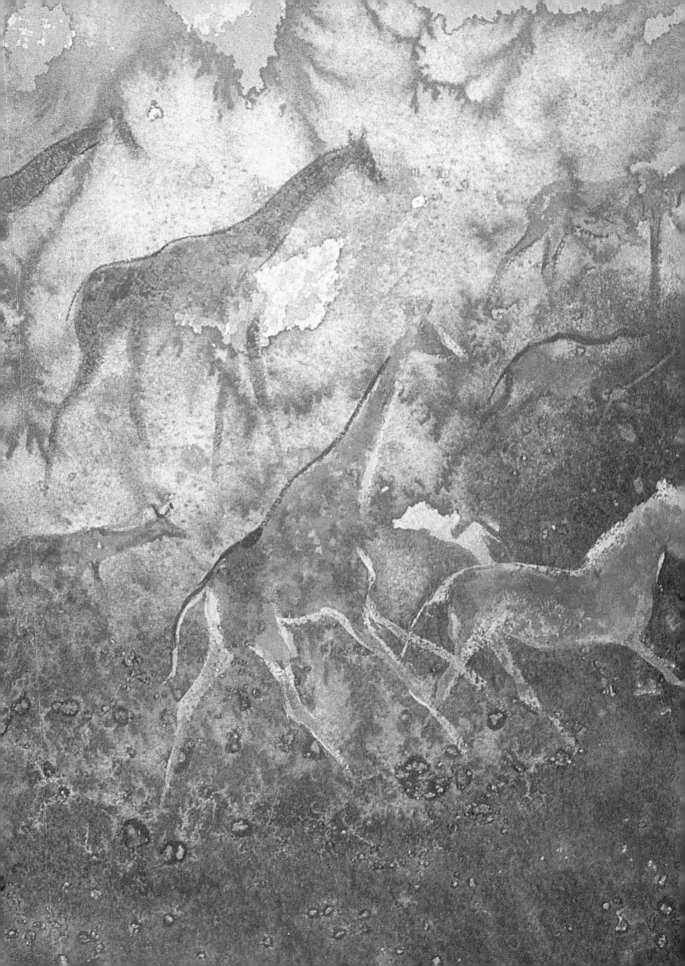

chapter 1

SUBJECT MATTERS

From the cave paintings of prehistory to the multiple images of the twentieth century mankind has never been short of something to paint. In a diverse and magnificent world we are inspired by both natural creation and man-made invention. Even the constant bombardment of images in the media has added to our visual repertoire. It is not just the picturesque that can move us to paint — everything and anything can interest us.

So how is it that, with all this pictorial wealth on offer, confrontation with a demanding sheet of all-too-white paper or a blank canvas often provokes the question in the aspiring artist's mind: 'What shall I paint?'.

MAKING THE DECISION

How do you decide what makes a good subject for a painting? You can rely on tried and tested themes, the timeless stalwarts that historically make good pictures: the bowl of fruit, the vase of flowers, the seated figure or portrait, or the classic view. But what about other ideas? Much around us, the details and small corners of wider aspects, the events that move us emotionally — these too are visually interesting, but not always immediately obvious as workable subjects for paintings.

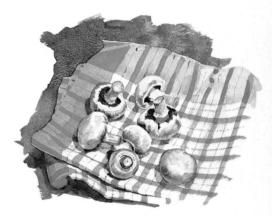

Do not seek—find!

PICASSO

OPPOSITE: **Rock Painting** (detail), *watercolour*

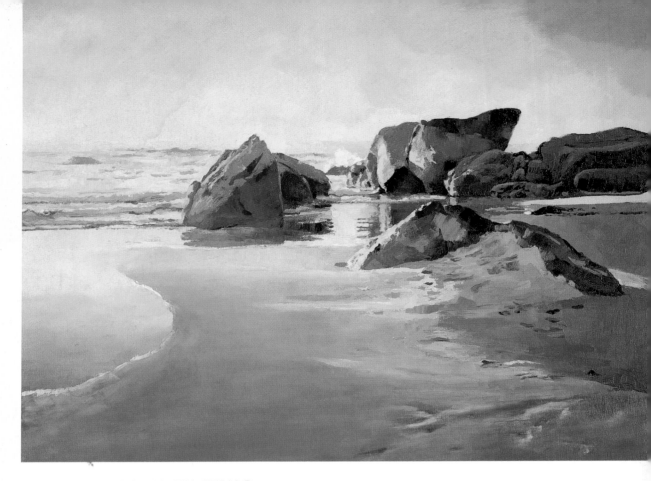

PAINTINGS-IN-WAITING

Most people probably believe there is nothing the artist cannot paint, but, even knowing this, still find it difficult to pick out from the view the features that will make a good painting. They may go in search of a subject but find it wanting in some way, or compose their picture without conviction because they are unsure of its worthiness as a subject for a painting.

In practice there are times when the desire to paint is strong but it is difficult to find a satisfactory grouping of objects or a perfectly composed view to act as the catalyst to get started. What is it that actually kindles a painter's interest?

THROUGH AN ARTIST'S EYES

The two-dimensional world of painting is a world of magical happenings. Painters lay colours, lines and shapes upon a flat surface and these are transformed into landscapes, people, objects and feelings. Understanding what makes this two-dimensional world tick is the key to the artist's vision.

If you view the world through eyes that fluently translate three dimensions into two dimensions you will be overwhelmed with painting ideas, and you will find the stimuli of the three-dimensional world increasing as your vision is enlarged. Your sense of colour and tone and perception of depth and space will gradually be heightened, making looking through the eyes an even greater pleasure than before.

In the Beginning

71 x 102 cm (28 x 40 in),
oil on canvas
Here just dabs of coloured oil paint are laid all over a piece of flat fabric, but you have no problem believing they represent a landscape. Look carefully at the rocks; they are made up of patches of reds, yellows, purples and blues, strange colours for rocks you might think, and yet they look perfectly natural.

OPPOSITE: **Counting Sheep**

13 x 20 cm (5 x 8 in), watercolour
If you are not particularly inspired by your surroundings try homing in on some small feature, such as I did with this broken piece of masonry in a Turkish yard. Fragments and snippets of a landscape make interesting subject matter for paintings and sketches.

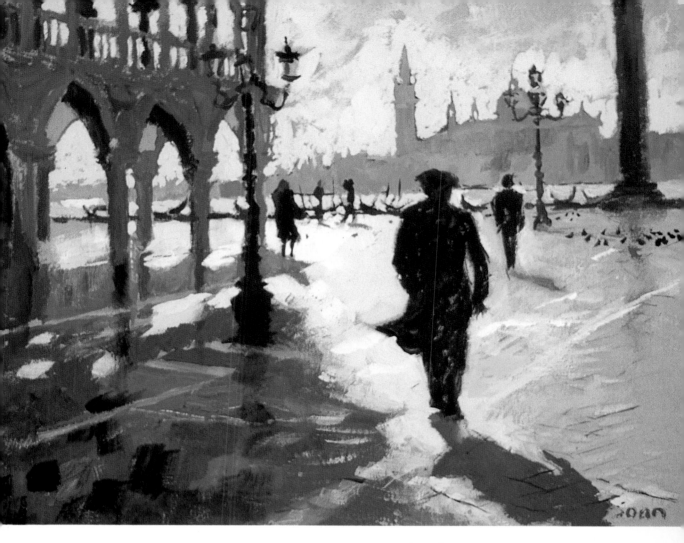

Crossing St Mark's Square

25 x 30 cm (10 x 12 in), oil on board
Dramatic light and strong
shadows were the inspiration for
this quick oil sketch on the back of
a sketchbook.

FINDING INSPIRATION

Painting starts with seeing. We are easily attracted to pleasant groupings of objects: an attractive composition in the landscape, the colours of flowers, a charming child or an interesting face. We are often struck by the effects of light and shadows.

The less tangible, such as an atmosphere, mood, or unusual incident, also engages the eye, while pattern, repetition and contrasts have strong visual appeal. Familiarity with the subject, a face we love, a memorable room, or even delicious food, can also stir us to reach for the paintbrushes.

Sometimes, however, inspiration is not always forthcoming. In those cases, instead of looking at the subject itself, you will need to look for the two-dimensional qualities sought by the picture plane: the nuances of light, line, shape, colour and incident. You will then find pictures everywhere. The aim of this book is to show you the elements that make up paintings, so that you can see them all around you and find a never-ending supply of subjects. In effect you will create your own inspiration.

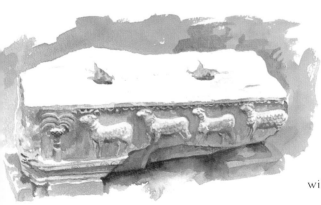

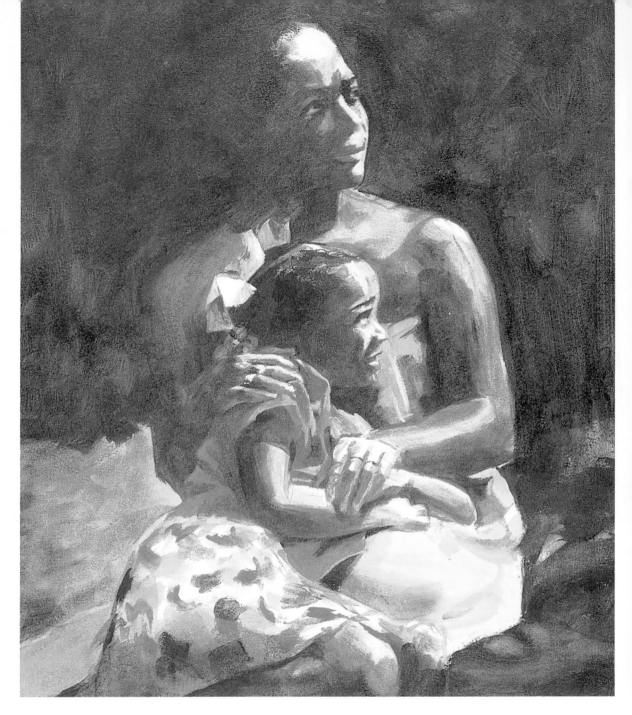

EMOTIONAL INPUT

Artists are inspired through their eyes, but inner emotion also plays a part. The thought behind the painting is as important as the physical subject. A subject may inspire us to paint because it holds some inner meaning not readily describable in words but suggested in the image. Painting has the power to convey this.

Zeal is a major factor in the making of a painting. The greater your interest in the subject the easier it is to paint. Your affection, enthusiasm or passion will be contained within the painting and will be felt by the viewer. The surface of a figurative painting is actually a convincing lie that aims to tell the truth.

Be My Shelter

76 x 60 cm (30 x 24 in),
acrylic on canvas
I wanted to evoke the vulnerability
of a child and the protection sought
in her mother's arms, and also hint
at the mother's own anxiety and
the comfort drawn from offering
protection. It is cumbersome to say
this in words, but the painting
implies it instantly.

To enable you to grasp the needs of a painting and then to find them as inspiration in the world around you, I have set this book out in three sections. The first section, 'The Quest', looks at the fundamental elements that make up a painting, what to look for in a subject and how to find it.

The second section, 'The Equipment', looks at what we paint with and the surfaces to which colour is applied. The medium will influence the outcome of the painting and can therefore have a bearing on your choice of subject. I have limited the scope of this book to the materials I use most often – watercolours, oils and occasionally acrylics – but most of what is said will apply to other media as well.

The third section, 'The Adventure', puts your new-found vision into practice. Each chapter relates to different environments encountered in our daily life or on our travels and explores some of the inexhaustible supply of subjects available as potential paintings.

At the end of many of the chapters there is a chance for you to put theory into practice with suggested projects. I also include some demonstrations. Soon you will find even the clutter on a table will inspire you to make a painting or the queue at the bus stop will excite you to open your sketchbook!

The January Sales

18 x 13 cm (7 x 5 in), watercolour
Moving subjects and swiftly changing light require a medium that is quick to apply and fast to dry. Watercolours on a small piece of khadi paper are the perfect choice of medium for this subject.

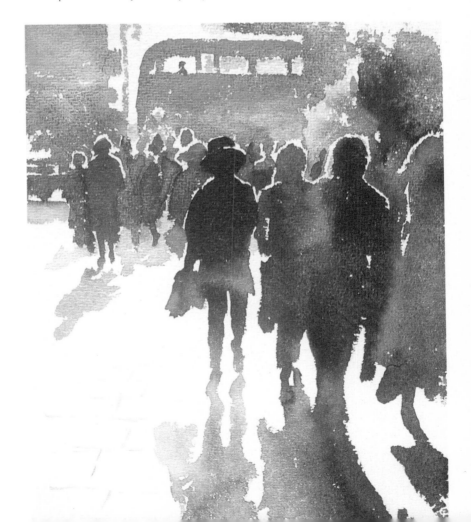

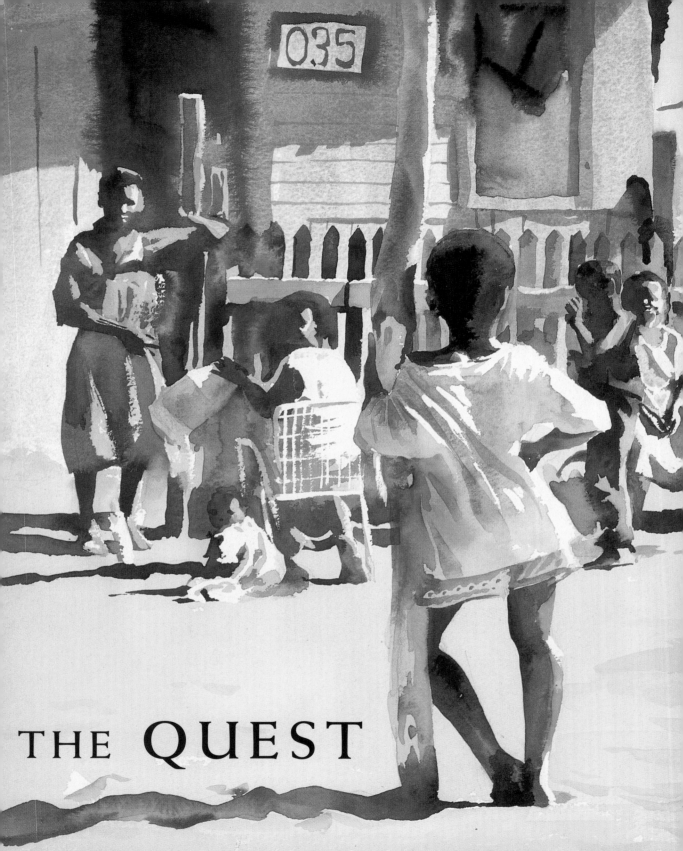

THE QUEST

WHAT TO LOOK FOR AND HOW TO FIND IT

Future Expectations, *43 x 56 cm (17 x 22 in), watercolour*

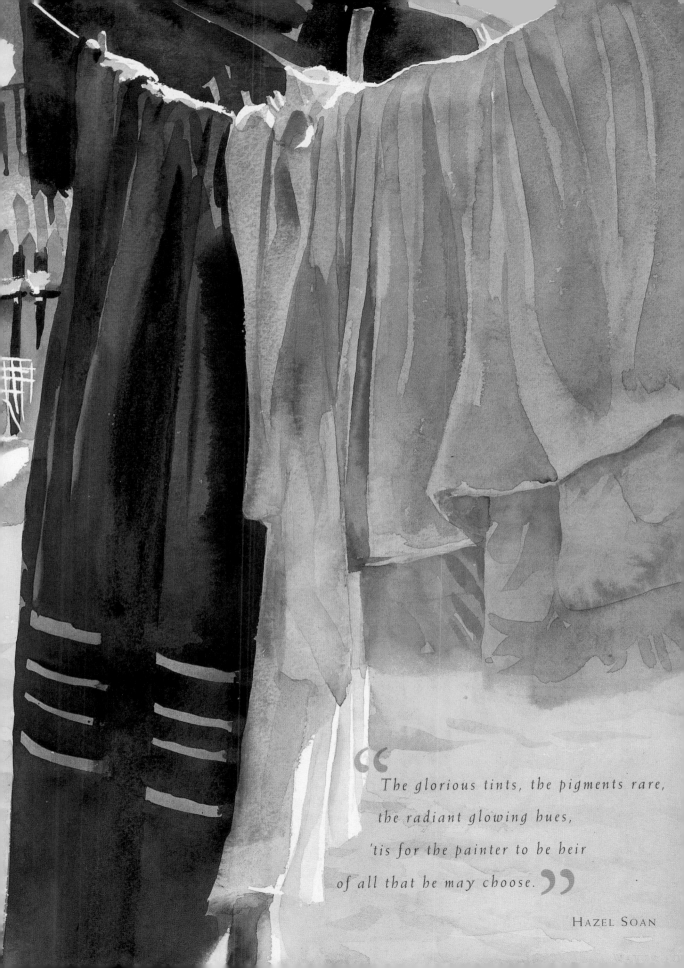

> *The glorious tints, the pigments rare,*
> *the radiant glowing hues,*
> *'tis for the painter to be heir*
> *of all that he may choose.*

HAZEL SOAN

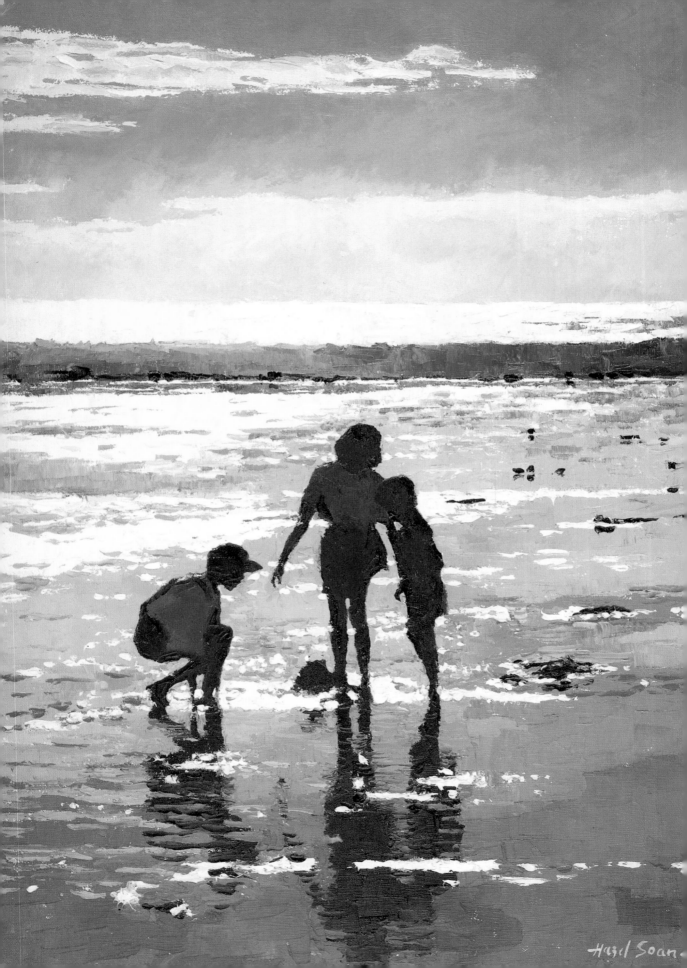

Hazel Soan

chapter 2

THE EYES HAVE IT

Painting starts with the eyes. There is a threefold pleasure and purpose in painting – the act of looking, the making of the painting, and the response to the outcome by others – but it all starts with seeing. In artistic terms this means grasping the components from a view that a painting requires.

Like exercise, the more you do the easier it becomes. So the more you look the more you are able to see. The more you notice things, the more you will want to paint. This facility may need encouragement to start, but once you have made the effort you will not want to stop. Training the eye to see is the first step.

THE ARTIST'S ARENA

The picture plane is the arena of the artist. The figurative painter convinces the viewer that three dimensions of unlimited proportion come to life within this shrunk and flattened space. Every centimetre of the picture plane is relative to the whole. Every line, shape or colour affects every other line, shape or colour across the flat surface.

You can practise seeing with an artist's eye even when you are not painting. After a short time it will become second nature and you may not even be aware of the shift.

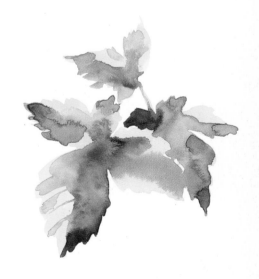

" ... the artist has only to trust his eyes. "

RODIN

OPPOSITE: **Digging for Treasure,** *76 x 56 cm (30 x 22 in), oil on canvas*

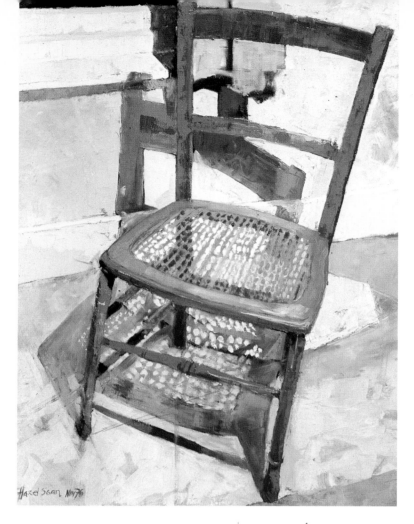

Hazel Soan Nov 96

The Studio Chair

*122 x 91 cm (48 x 36 in),
oil on canvas*
*This painting is composed around
the shapes of the spaces between the
wooden rungs of the chair. To make
it easier to draw shapes in
proportion use the length of an
outstretched pencil to compare the
widths of the space-shapes with
their heights.*

THINKING TWO-DIMENSIONALLY

The things that make interesting paintings are not necessarily interesting subjects per se but groups of elements that form a particular set of shapes, colours or tones that the artist recognizes will make a successful composition or colour scheme upon the flat picture surface. This is not to deny the emotional input of the subject, but for an image to work as a painting it must meet the needs of the two-dimensional world.

In material reality the image on the picture plane is just a pattern of shapes and colours, but in total reality paintings are persuasive and evocative, with a life of their own.

GETTING IN SHAPE

The simplest way to train the eye to see is to look at shapes and outlines. On the flat surface of a painting it is easy to realize that the shapes of spaces between parts are going to be as important as the shapes of objects themselves. Yet so often these shapes are barely observed. The proportion of those space-shapes is also crucial to determine their outlines.

Look at the spaces under chairs and tables, the gap between an arm and the trunk of the body, the space inside the handle of a jug. Observe the spaces under tree canopies.

The Neighbour's Garage

*20 x 25 cm (8 x 10 in),
half-finished watercolour*
*These early stages show that one
tone includes the garage walls, the
shadow on the drive and the roof,
the shady parts of trees and even
the garden gate, but they are
painted as just two organic shapes.*

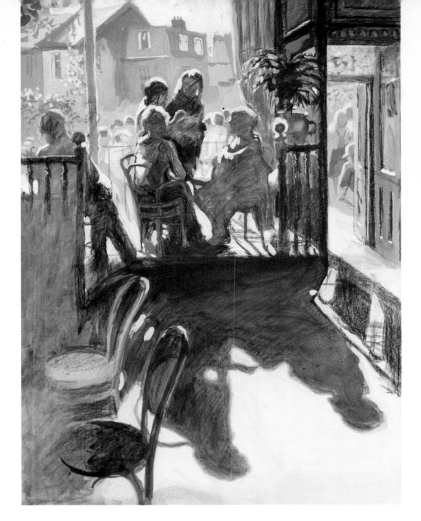

Long Shadows in Parsons Green

71 x 46 cm (28 x 18 in), watercolour, gouache and conté crayon on paper
Once you start to see in shapes, drawing becomes much easier. Perspective falls into place because, instead of guessing the different angles of receding lines, the lines are found from the angled sides of the shapes they bound. Again use the length of the pencil to find relative proportion between near and far objects.

THE SHAPE OF THINGS

Now start observing the shapes of the items themselves. See their height and width, their overall proportion, not the surface features.

Try to outline the correct shapes, or block them in with flat brushstrokes from the inside out. Alternatively, create their shapes by painting only the shapes that surround them.

Next look at group shapes – a cluster of trees, a knot of people, for example. Do not limit your eye to individual items; look for shapes of the same tone or colour. For example, there may be a dark shape under the eaves of a house that includes a door, a window, a shadow and half of a bush, or the skirt of a seated woman may merge with the chair and both may merge into the shadow on the wall. For the artist these united shapes become one item on the flat picture plane.

ASSUME NOTHING

A bobbing head is the mark of an observant eye. Constantly refer to the source of your visual information. Never presume you know what anything looks like, no matter how familiar – on few occasions will the light falling on your subject be repeated in exactly the same way. Observe it as you have never seen it before and that freshness of vision will translate into your paintings.

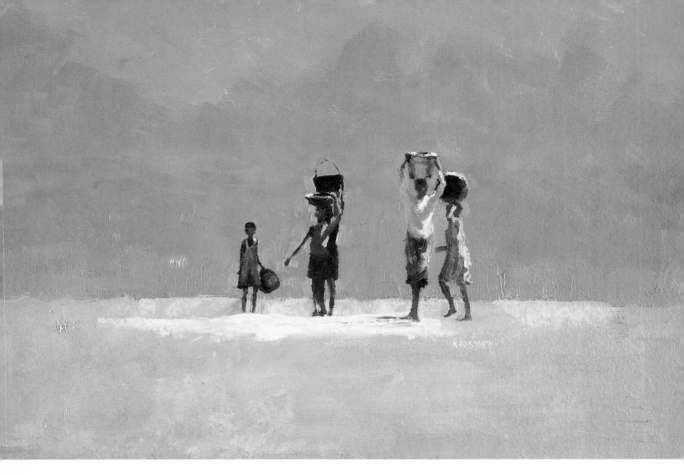

SIMPLIFICATION

When you look at the world you do not notice or see every detail. You pick out that which interests you and catches your eye. A camera cannot be selective about what it sees, but the artist can be, and it is this very selection of what really matters to you that makes a painting original.

If the shape of a group of objects has attracted you – a huddle of buildings on a skyline, perhaps – it is this that becomes your subject. If you forget this and get carried away with putting too much detail in the brickwork, for example, you run the risk of losing the essence of your painting. The more you can synthesize the particular elements that interest you the stronger your painting is likely to be.

FRAGMENTS OF THE WHOLE

When observing the view with a painting in mind let the eye roam back and forth, left and right to find scenes within scenes within scenes. Clarification may involve homing in on tiny features and sometimes your subject is a fragment of the whole. A tuft of grass on a dune can say as much about a beach as a painting of the entire shore; a pair of shoes may hint more at a person's character than a full-length portrait; a corner of a table in an interior may be more interesting as an image than painting the whole room.

ABOVE: **Day by Day**
20 x 28 cm (8 x 11 in), oil on canvas
In reality this particular stretch of beach on Lake Malawi was more cluttered. I simplified the scene to impart the spirit of the task I had watched performed day by day along the lake.

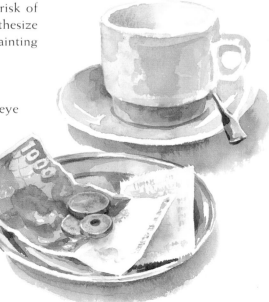

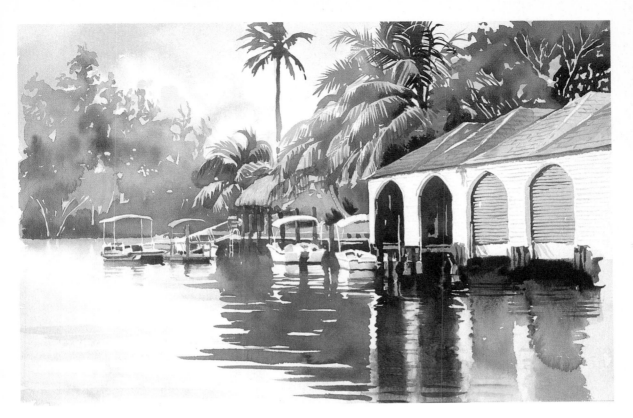

Everglades

38 x 56 cm (15 x 22 in), watercolour

It is the artist's prerogative to pick and choose from any subject whatever interests them. Other things were happening in this view, but I included only the elements I wanted to paint. The resulting image has a stronger impact, and will be clearer to read by the beholder.

OPPOSITE: 'La Cuenta, Por Favor'

20 x 20 cm (8 x 8 in), watercolour

Idling over a cup of coffee on holiday I noticed how interesting the money looked upon the plate, a tiny fragment from amongst the whole scene of the marina, but it provided a delightful subject for a 30-minute sketch and much amusement for the waiters.

DISTILLING THE SUBJECT

Sometimes the desired subject seems just too daunting to tackle. It may be a vast panorama, a busy street scene, a complicated building or a detailed fabric. To resolve this, stand back, half close your eyes and look for the most obvious lights and darks, and the main lines and shapes. Concentrate on portraying these. Simplification will strengthen the painting, not weaken it.

In the course of painting you may get carried away with details and forget to see the image as a whole. Holding on to your subject can sometimes be as hard as finding the right subject in the first place! Be single minded. Ask yourself, 'What did I first notice when I was drawn to this scene?', 'What makes it exciting?'. Keep this initial inspiration in mind to prevent yourself from overworking the painting and losing your way.

GETTING INVOLVED

We all have different passions and emotions. Do not be afraid to record visually the objects and incidents that provoke your interest. The seemingly obscure statements made by small details may be far more meaningful than a fully composed view.

Through painting you become acquainted with your subject. After you have finished painting a landscape or interior, walk into it and enjoy this familiarity. Touch the tree you have lovingly painted for the last hour, handle the objects on which you bestowed your time. This intimacy is an added bonus that many painters forget to enjoy as they pack up their paints and walk away.

OVER TO YOU...

Training the eye to see does not happen overnight. Practise by observing and drawing shapes and distilling the elements of a subject to its essentials, using any medium you wish. Do not judge yourself on results — remember you are learning to see, not making paintings.

Motto
Most said with
minimum means.

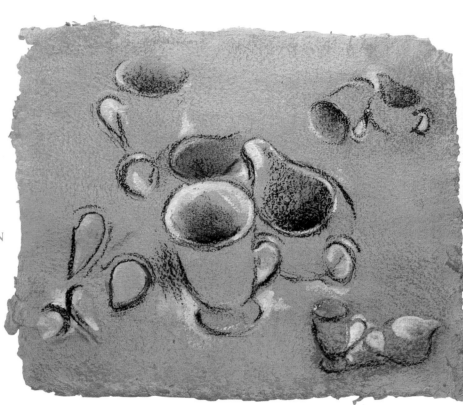

▶ **THE SPACES WITHIN**
charcoal and acrylic
In the first exercise observe and draw the spaces inside cups and jugs and their handles. Draw the shape of the spaces rather than drawing the items or handles themselves. I have used charcoal and white acrylic on stained paper.

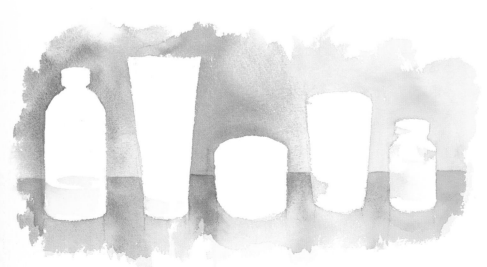

◀ **THE SPACES BETWEEN**
watercolour
For the second exercise pick a group of objects from the bathroom cupboard. Place the items in a line with gaps between them. Paint just the spaces in between and around the items. Be aware of the distances across each item to the next space. Aim to describe the items only by the spaces around them and you will find the items will appear as if by magic!

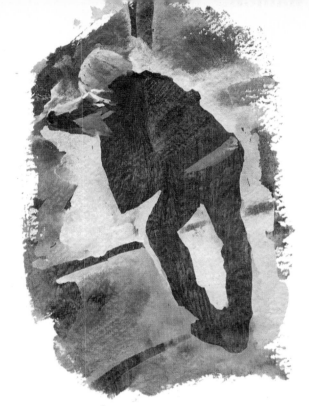

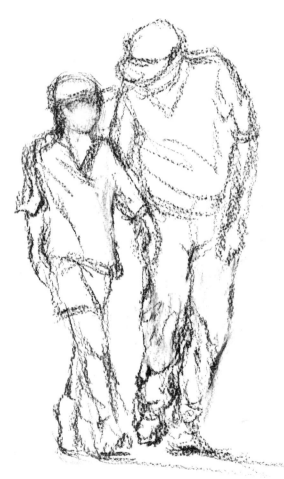

◀ THE OVERALL SHAPE
acrylic

For the third exercise place an object or figure so that they are silhouetted against a light background. Wash over your page with dark colours. I painted an acrylic wash of blues and browns over the paper. When it is dry block in the areas around the shape of your object with white paint. Do not draw an outline, but try to see the surrounding shape.

▼ FINDING THE ESSENCE OF THE SUBJECT
charcoal

Lastly, find a picture of something that stirs your emotions. I chose a photograph of a father leaning down to his son; the guiding link of hands seemed to represent fatherhood.

Draw the image onto your paper looking only at the subject and not down at the page. Use scribbly lines back and forth over areas until you feel you have familiarized yourself with the subject. Resist the temptation to look at your drawing. When you have finished you will probably be horrified at the muddle on the page, but now start again.

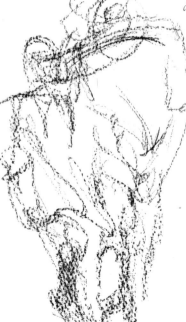

▲ *This time you can look at your drawing while you try in a few meaningful strokes to distil from the image the lines you think best describe its meaning.*

POSTSCRIPT

Follow these exercises by drawing the spaces under chairs and tables, the intervals between tree trunks and spaces under tree canopies. Always check that the height, width and proportion of the space corresponds to what you see.

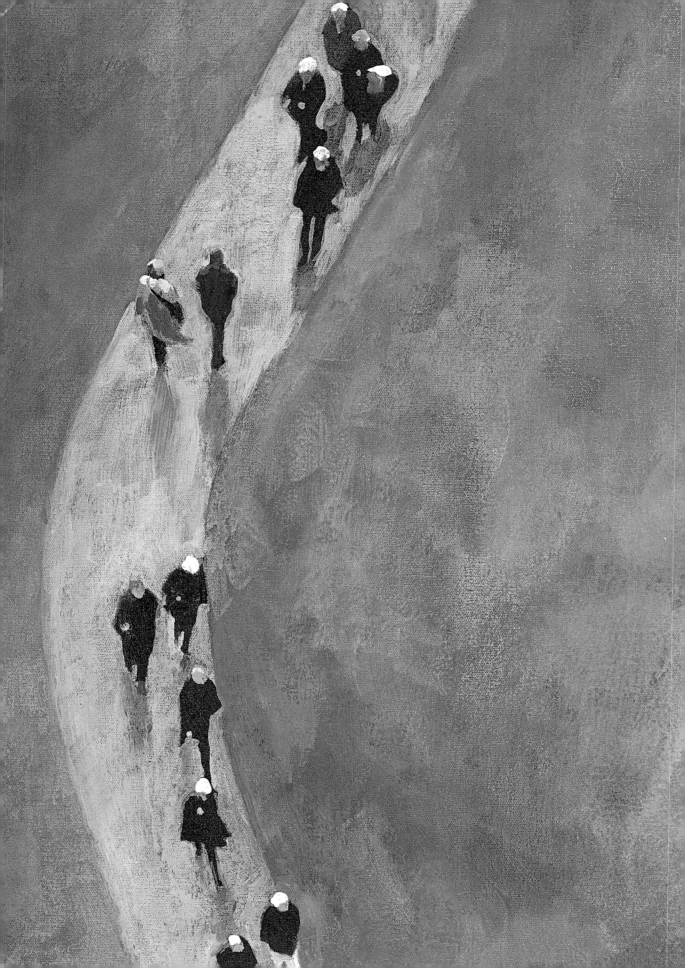

chapter 3

DISCOVERING
COMPOSITION

Every picture has a boundary that is determined by the limits of the surface on which it is painted. The actual painting takes place within that perimeter, though it need not fill it, and the effect of the painting may be to extend well beyond. Good composition is fundamental; it is inspired by the subject matter, but not ruled by it.

Naturally good compositions occur all around us, though they are not always readily apparent. Somewhere within the scene is the painting-in-waiting; recognizing it and translating it onto paper is the art of composition. This simply means being aware of a workable set of shapes, lines, colours and tones that, grouped together, make an interesting pattern on the picture surface.

FINDING THE PAINTING

Obviously picturesque views would appear to make good paintings, and often there is a sense of obligation to paint them, but they may not immediately have what a painting needs to be interesting. The artist must therefore either jiggle the view around or perhaps take a small part of the view that provides a more satisfactory composition.

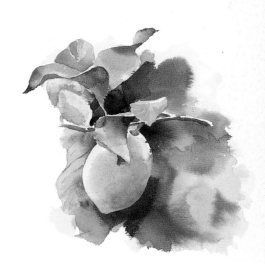

The composition is the organized sum of the interior functions (expressions) of every part of the work.

KANDINSKY

OPPOSITE: **View from the London Eye,** 43 x 28 cm (17 x 11 in), acrylic on canvas

READYMADE COMPOSITIONS

A satisfying, asymmetrical, but balanced, arrangement of shapes, colours and tones are the usual elements of a successful composition. If the composition of a painting is well arranged you will find it easier to make the painting work, but this does not mean compositions need to be harmoniously balanced, or overly planned. Jarring or obscure arrangements make interesting compositions too. All you need is an awareness of what will work on the two-dimensional picture plane.

THE SOURCE

If you have control over the physical elements you are painting, as in a still life or portrait, you can move parts of the actual subject around until the arrangement pleases the eye. It is easier to glean your shapes, colours and tones direct from the source than to make wild guesses about what might look better.

In the landscape it is not always possible to find perfect compositions – few of us can move mountains! Sometimes you must sacrifice literal truth for pictorial success. Always remember the painting lives on independently of the source of its inspiration. Even if your painting intends to be a truthful record of the view, it may be necessary for the painting's sake to make alterations to the composition; move trees closer together or leave out a few fields. Free yourself from the obligation to paint everything in front of you; that is not a recipe for success.

Transition

20 x 28 cm (8 x 11 in), oil on board
The horizontal division of a sky-meets-land composition is a good starting point. In this painting the horizon is placed above the centre line to avoid dividing the painting in half, and the line of rocks to the right is balanced by the centre left rock coming slightly forward.

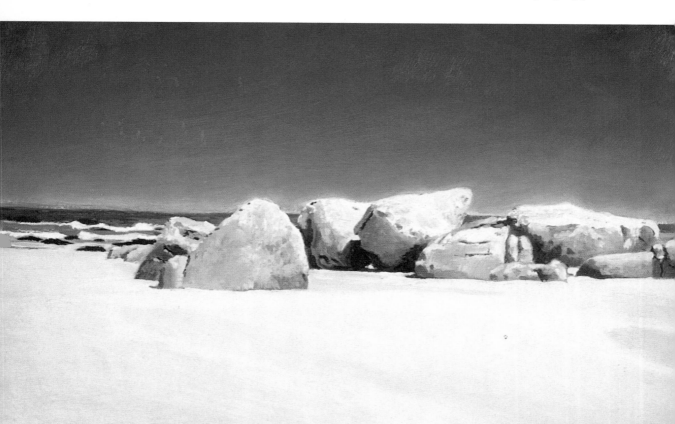

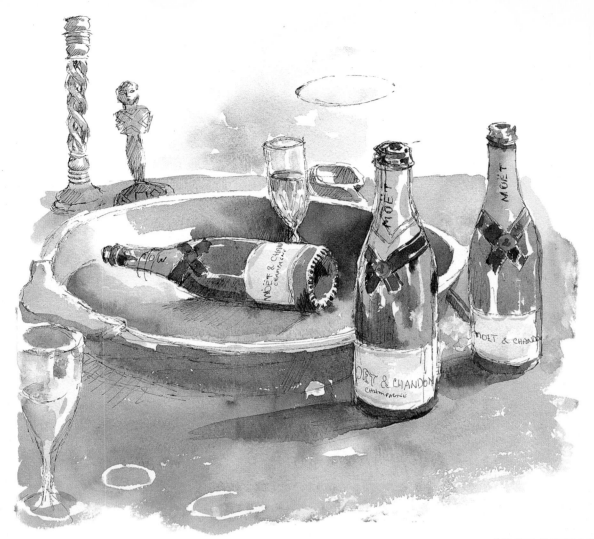

The morning after the night before, 1. 1. 2000

20 x 20 cm (8 x 8 in),
watercolour and ink
Bleary-eyed after celebrating the
entry into the new millennium, I
could not resist painting the debris
of bottles. The composition is
hopelessly unbalanced, but the
sentiment is strong and the sketch
remains as a good New Year
memory. Is that not a good enough
reason for a painting?

SKETCHING

Filling a sketchbook with ideas before embarking on a painting enables you to respond quickly to the inspiration of your subject and to find out what really interests you, without having to worry about planning your composition. These immediate unplanned images are often the most exhilarating work of an artist, and it is worth remembering that it is also possible to over-compose a painting to the point where predictability kills off its life. Pay heed to your sketchbook; it can teach you much about how you see and what excites you.

HOW TO COMPOSE

To find the two-dimensional layout of the three-dimensional world look through a viewfinder. I often use my index fingers and thumbs to make a frame, but the best way is to hold two L-shaped pieces of card together, forming an empty space in the middle. You can make any rectilinear shape to suit the view or the painting.

As you look through the viewfinder move it around until you find the best layout within the rectangular space. Half close your eyes so that you can see tonal balance and relative shapes.

THE FOCAL POINT

Usually the subject of your painting will be the focal point, the place in the painting you wish to draw the viewer's eye towards. Sometimes, of course, the subject is intangible – an atmosphere or an emotion – but there may still be an area of the painting, large or small, that you wish to emphasize.

If the subject of your painting is a particular feature place its position within the boundary of the composition before drawing the peripherals. There is nothing more dispiriting than drawing a picture starting from the edges, only to find the main feature is too far over to one side and you have to start all over again.

To simplify drawing the composition imagine there is a pane of glass held vertically in the viewfinder. This is your picture plane. Trace the main shapes and lines of the view onto this imaginary glass. Point your finger into the middle to find a central reference and work out from there.

FLOW LINES AND REPETITION

Within your view look for lines that lead the eye from the edge of the composition towards the main features or focal point, or lines that lead the eye out from the centre of the painting to the perimeter and beyond. Notice other lines that repeat or echo the lines of the main feature. These emphasize your focus of interest, though you may not even realize that they have attracted you until

OPPOSITE: **Boatboy**

33 x 46 cm (13 x 18 in), oil on paper
The elements that lead to a focal point are a guide for the eye. Here the viewer's eye travels from the dazzling sun into the prow of the boat, along the hull and up into the boy. His oar then leads us smartly down into the water. But we could also enter from the right and zigzag along the ripples of the water up into the boat.

Breakfast on the Terrace

43 x 58 cm (17 x 23 in), watercolour
A lot is happening in this painting, but by organizing the composition of the items in the foreground the background activity could be painted in with more abandon.

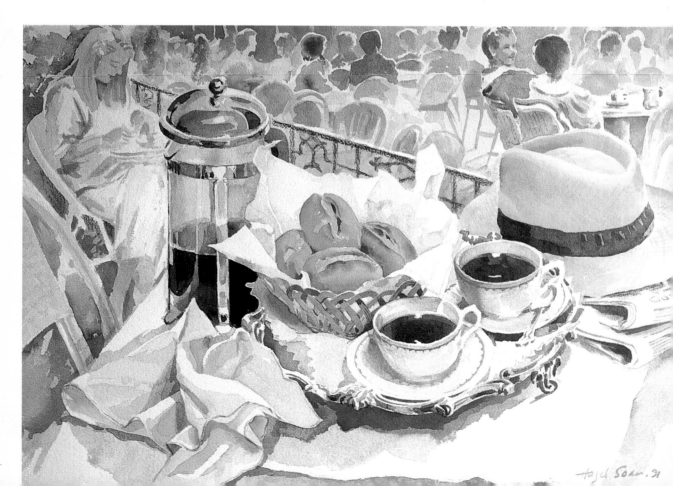

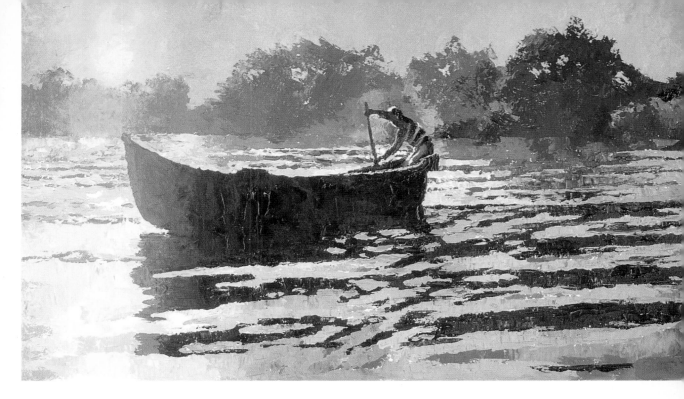

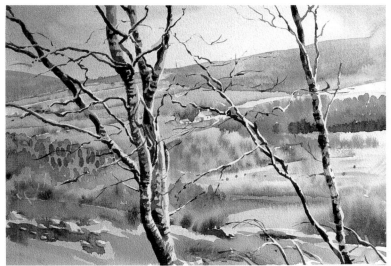

RIGHT: **Wicklow Mountains**

25 x 30 cm (10 x 12 in), watercolour
Look at the strong vertical parallels of the foreground tree trunks and branches and the gentle contrast of horizontal parallelograms made by the distant field patterns. When choosing your viewpoint look for these natural rhythms that occur in the landscape.

you draw the composition on the picture surface. Examples could be the direction of a pathway echoed in the rhythm of some branches, the edges of items on a table converging to one common point, or the position of limbs paralleled in the folds of clothes.

Repetition of a shape can also make an interesting composition. In the painting above the V-shaped spaces between the limbs of the trees are repeated several times to good effect.

There are no rules in painting, but generally horizon lines are better placed above and below the centre line, and main features not placed dead centre. In reality your subject may be a particular item, but in painting its existence will rely on something to do with its shape, colour or tone, an adjacent shadow, or a space in between items. Think two-dimensionally.

OVER to YOU...

Now it is your turn to discover the potential compositions in your immediate vicinity. Use a viewfinder if it helps and do not be embarrassed to be seen looking through your framed fingers. Any medium will do. I have used oils on paper and a size 9 brush.

Motto
If in doubt,
leave it out.

▶ REPETITION WITHIN AN IMAGE
Look for reflections and multiples of an object. Repetition within a view draws items together, as with these sun-loungers reflected in the water of a pool.

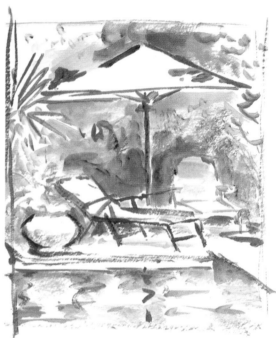

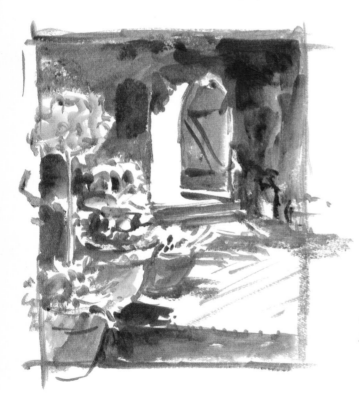

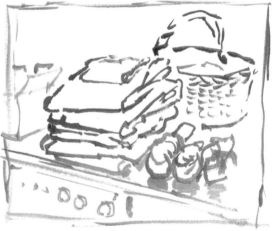

BALANCE OF LIGHT AND DARK TONES
A contrast of tones can be used as a strong compositional device in a picture. Light coming through a garden gateway can look more dramatic than a quiet, even light.

ITEMS IN RELATION TO EACH OTHER
Go round your home and garden and find some readymade compositions. Draw quickly, but place the items accurately in relation to each other on the page. A pile of ironing provides interesting shapes.

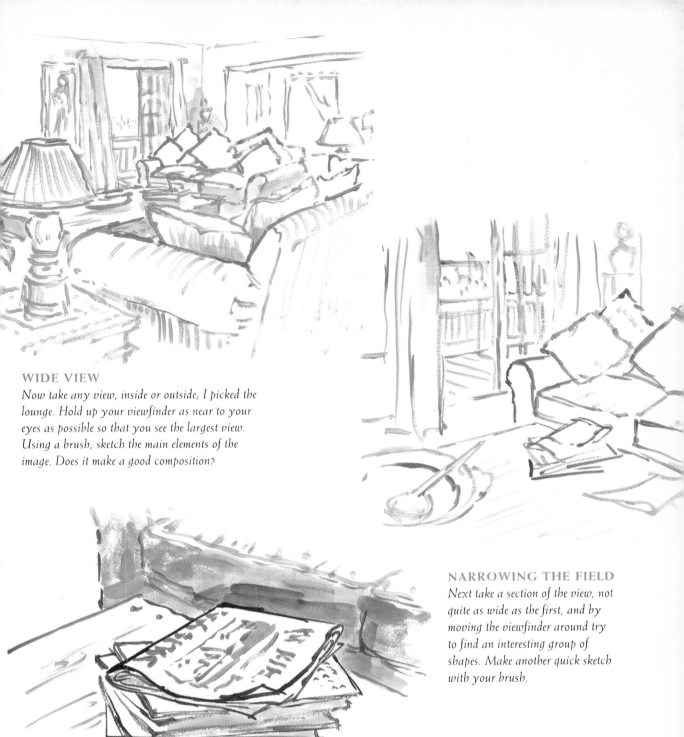

WIDE VIEW
Now take any view, inside or outside; I picked the lounge. Hold up your viewfinder as near to your eyes as possible so that you see the largest view. Using a brush, sketch the main elements of the image. Does it make a good composition?

NARROWING THE FIELD
Next take a section of the view, not quite as wide as the first, and by moving the viewfinder around try to find an interesting group of shapes. Make another quick sketch with your brush.

CLOSING IN ON A DETAIL
Finally, go in close on a detail within the view, and make a quick sketch noting the light and dark balance. I chose the pile of magazines on the coffee table.

POSTSCRIPT
You can check the strength and balance of your composition by looking at the sketch reflected in a mirror. If you are unhappy with it start again.

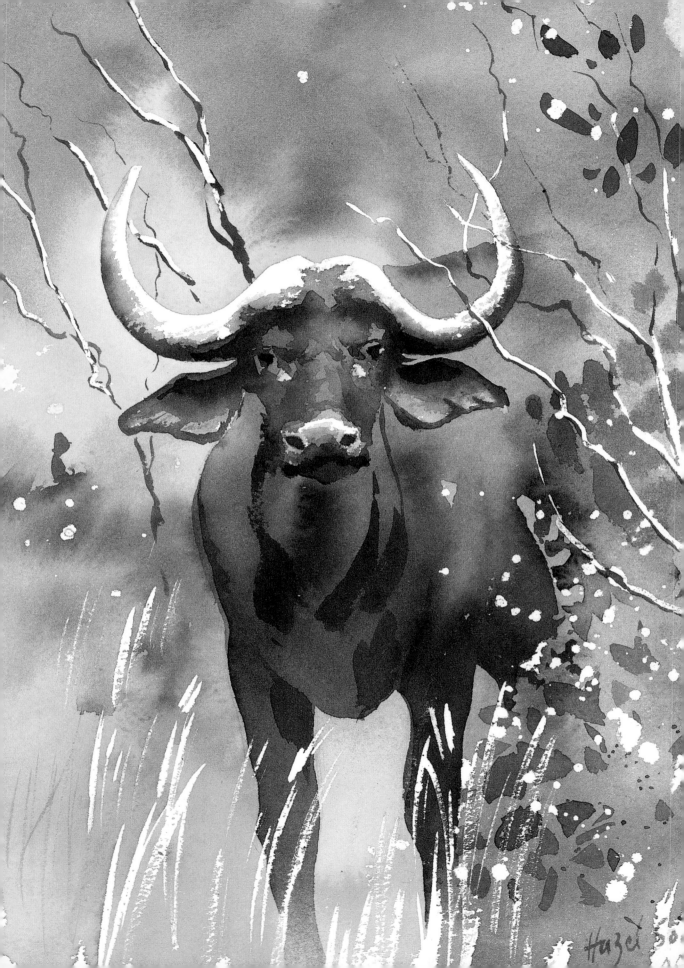

chapter 4

RESPONDING TO COLOUR

Colour, with all its cheerful connotations, is often the inspiration for a painting. But it is not just the bright colours of flowers, clothing or sunsets that attract the eye. The muted colours playing across a landscape, the subtle nuances of a complexion or the greys of urban drizzle are equally enthralling for the artist to paint.

There is probably no natural colour you find unattractive and even the contemporary colours of the plastic world have their own garish charm. So with all this wealth of colour around how can you choose? How can you guess what will translate well into a painting and how faithful do you need to be in copying the colours you see?

THE PICTURE PLANE

The answers are once again found in the two-dimensional world of the picture. Your painting may look like a view across a valley or a group of children at play, but in reality it is a collection of colours playing across a flat surface, be it canvas, paper or board. It needs to work as a painting first, separate from its inspiration, to truthfully tell the tale of the interest you felt in the subject.

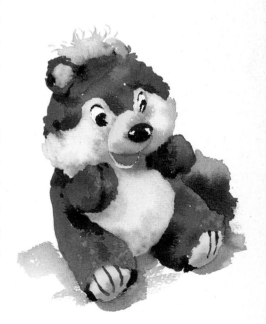

" *Give me mud and I will paint you the flesh of Venus.* "

DELACROIX

OPPOSITE: **Voyeur,** *28 x 20 cm (11 x 8 in), watercolour*

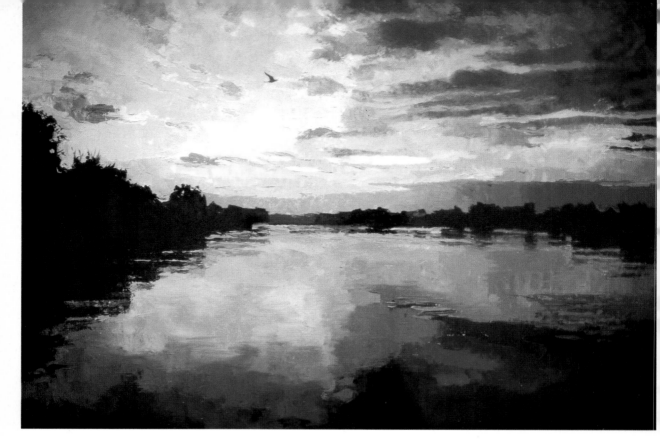

COLOURFUL BEHAVIOUR

Colour is relative, since every colour changes depending on the combination of colours around it. Under a different light source, such as sunlight, cloud cover or artificial light, colours vary quite dramatically. These factors alone free you from the obligation to copy colours exactly. Unless you are able to copy every colour absolutely perfectly and under one light source, at one time, any aberration in any colour in the painting will affect all the others and veracity is made null and void.

So, you are not bound to an exactitude of colour. You can use colour to actually enhance your painting. You can take what you see and, if necessary, exaggerate or mute colours to make the painting stronger. Many subjects that might not appeal immediately because the colours seem dull are no longer ruled out if you can see the tiny differences between variations of colour.

INTERACTION OF COLOUR

All colours, except the pure primaries of red, yellow and blue, are made up of two or three of those colours. A colour that contains just two of the primaries looks brighter and stronger if placed next to the third, and these colours are termed opposite or complementary colours. Orange (a mixture of red and yellow) will appear a brighter orange if placed next to its opposite, blue, than if it is placed next to a red, yellow or green.

So if you want to bring out the richness of an orange flower in a painting, or a wonderful head of auburn hair, paint a blue or bluish version of a colour next to the flower or around the head.

Sunrise on the Danube Delta

56 x 76 cm (22 x 30 in), oil on paper
Red and turquoise, yellow and purple, blue and orange — each of these combinations are complementary colours. By using them together in the painting they make each colour appear stronger and brighter, creating the clean radiance of sunrise.

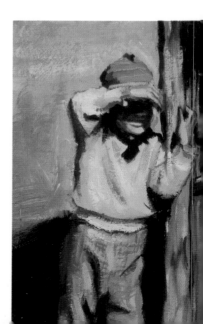

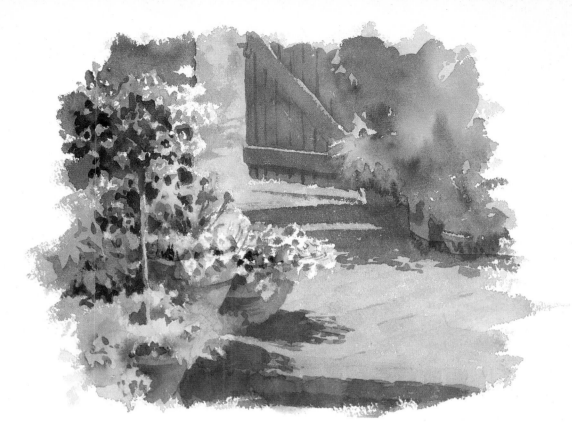

The Patio

23 x 28 cm (9 x 11 in), watercolour
The Burnt Sienna of the patio looks very orange. By adding blue, the complementary colour into the shadows, the orange can be muted. There is a wash of Burnt Sienna and touches of Cadmium Red under the foliage to dull down the greens and prevent them making the pots look too red.

OPPOSITE: **Hide and Seek**

18 x 13 cm (7 x 5 in), oil on board
In the man-made world contrasts of opposites often occur in clothing combinations. In this painting the yellow jersey vies strongly with its complementary purple-blue trousers, and a paler version of the colour is used in the background to brighten the yellow even more.

NATURAL OPPOSITES

Opposite colours are called complementary colours because added together they make up the full complement of three primaries. In the natural world we can find numerous complementary colour contrasts, often in the floral kingdom and between skies and landscapes.

A colour contrast makes a great subject to paint. A dialogue of two contrasting coloured areas dominating the picture surface, such as beach and sky, make a strong image. Look out for them in their more subtle, less obvious forms as well, when the colours are yellow-ochres, red-browns and blue-greys.

USING COLOURS

In painting we can use the interaction of opposite colours to enhance and detract. By mixing a complementary colour with its opposite we can gradually turn it towards browns and greys.

A colour will push an adjacent colour away from itself towards its opposite. This comparative effect is common to most things in life; for instance, a tall person next to a short person will make the tall person appear taller and the short person seem shorter. A red next to an orange will force the orange to look more yellow, pushing it away from red around the colour circle towards green.

When we see the effects of comparisons around us colours leap out from their surroundings. Red flowers, for example, look richer on dull days than in warm sunlight as the surrounding cool dull greens push them deeper into the warmth of red. A mauve cloud will make the sky around it appear more blue.

ALTERED COLOUR

The perceived colours of objects are altered by tinted and reflected light. The white of a boat hull lit by the yellow/orange light of sunset is tinted a golden yellow, while the shadows cast by ropes and fenders take on a complementary blue. Light or shiny-surfaced items reflect brightly coloured adjacent objects. A red tomato on a white kitchen top shares its colour with the surface beneath. As you paint you will notice this happening in more subtle forms. Look for ideas on polished wood, crockery, against white cloth, on newspapers and alongside any reflective or wet surfaces.

COLOUR AND MOOD

Colour also has temperature; for instance, red is a warm colour and blue is cool. Reds, yellows and oranges, light bright tones and energetic brushstrokes bestow a cheerful upbeat mood on paintings. More subtle warm colours and tones tend to be uplifting rather than vivacious. Jarring colour combinations among vivid colours combined with brusque brushmarks can even suggest anger.

Christmas at the Ritz Club
20 x 20 cm (8 x 8 in), watercolour
Lamplight and firelight bathe the room with a warm yellow glow. Yellow Ochre is the perfect colour for this warm light.

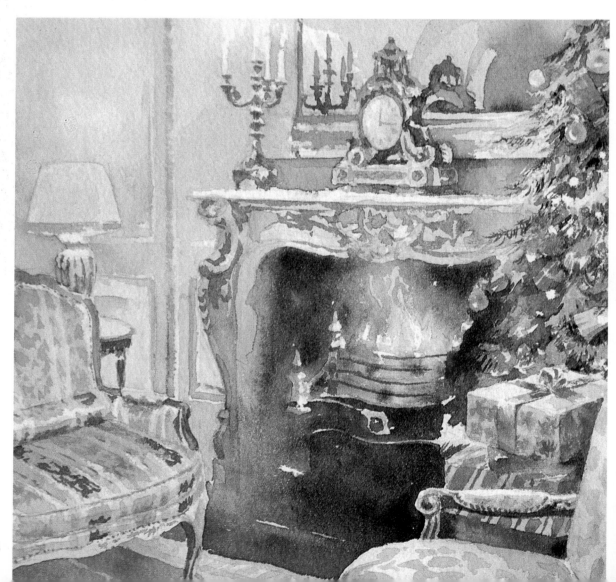

In the Morning Light

38 x 28 cm (15 x 11 in), oil on paper
This painting is almost all blue with just a few dashes of yellow in the areas of light. The mood created by the blues is easier to read in paint than to put into words; it evokes both tenderness and vulnerability without being in the least depressing.

Cool colours, especially blues, evoke calm, restraint and even melancholy. If you wish a subject to be serious or peaceful look for the blues within the view, and if you want warmth and *joie de vivre* seek out oranges, warm yellows and reds. Emphasize these with their complementaries.

Dark tones herald mystery, and strong contrasts suggest drama and denote hardship. Sombre colours and cheerless greys spell gloom and adversity.

To assess temperature look carefully at each colour in relation to the one next to it. Ask yourself, 'Is this colour redder or bluer than that one, even by the tiniest amount?', 'Is it colder or warmer?'. It is these differences in colours, one against another, that build any subject into an interesting painting.

OVER TO YOU...

One of the best ways to see colours for painting is to assess the temperature of a colour by asking yourself if it veers towards red, the warm side of the spectrum, or towards blue, the cool side. In an ideal palette you will probably have a cool and a warm version of each colour. All colours illustrated in the swatches are watercolour.

Motto
Be bold.

COLOUR SWATCHES

Here is a suggested palette of colours that includes one warm and one cool colour of each hue for you to practise with.

WARM

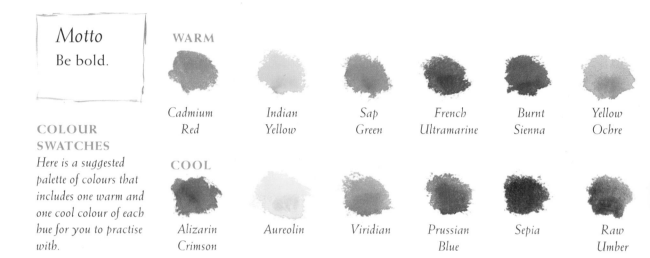

| Cadmium Red | Indian Yellow | Sap Green | French Ultramarine | Burnt Sienna | Yellow Ochre |

COOL

| Alizarin Crimson | Aureolin | Viridian | Prussian Blue | Sepia | Raw Umber |

ORANGE COLOUR MIX

To make bright colours from two different hues it is necessary to mix two near primary colours of the same temperature. This bright orange is made with Cadmium Red and Indian Yellow, both warm versions of their colours.

For a slightly less bright colour, mix together two colours of different temperatures. This orange is made from Alizarin Crimson and Indian Yellow. It is less bright because Alizarin Crimson contains a touch of blue; therefore the mixed colour contains all three primaries.

Here two cool versions of warm colours are mixed together, Alizarin Crimson and Aureolin, making a cooler, less bright orange, as the involvement of all three primaries moves the colour gently towards black.

GREEN COLOUR MIX

Here is a similar set of colour swatches using the warm and cool versions of blues and yellows to make greens.

Try to guess the two-colour combinations used in each case. The answers can be found below each swatch.

The brightest green is made from Aureolin and Prussian Blue (two cool colours).

A less bright green is mixed from Indian Yellow and Prussian Blue (a warm colour and a cool colour).

A dull green results from mixing Indian Yellow and French Ultramarine (two warm colours).

PURPLE COLOUR MIX

The brightest version will be made from a red leaning to blue, Alizarin Crimson, plus a blue leaning to red, French Ultramarine.

A duller mauve is made from two cool versions of colours, Alizarin Crimson and Prussian Blue.

A mix of French Ultramarine and Cadmium Red is duller still as the Cadmium Red begins to lean towards the yellow side of the spectrum (three primaries involved).

Prussian Blue (cool blue leaning to yellow) plus Cadmium Red (warm red leaning to yellow) lose the purple but make a lovely dark tone.

POSTSCRIPT

Remember colour is relative.
All the oranges are warm colours in relation to blue, but there are cool versions of warm colours and vice versa.

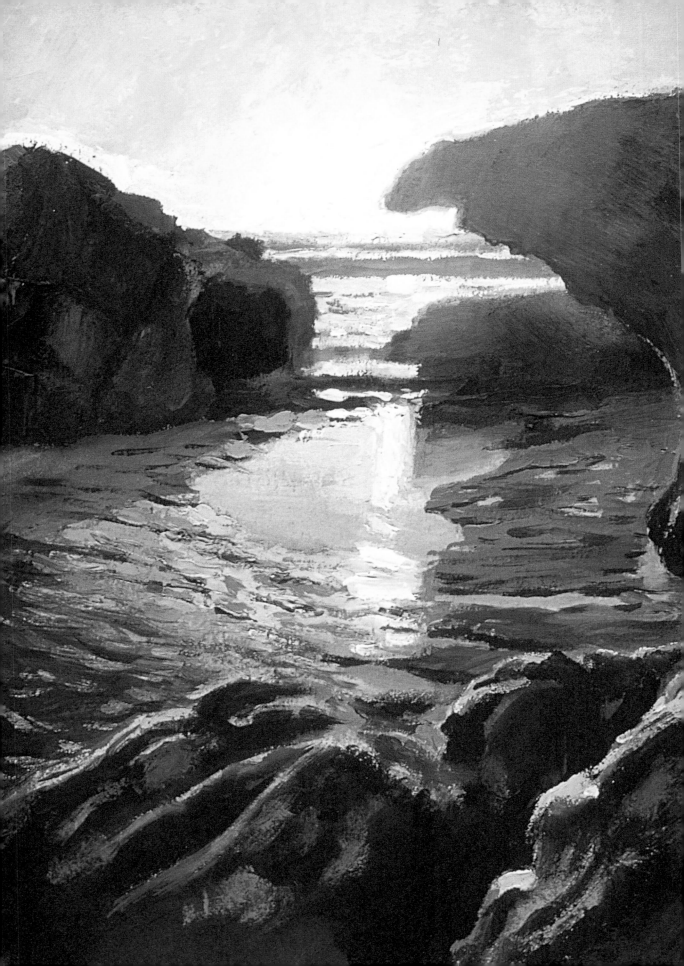

VALUING TONE

Colour may be a great inspiration, but tone is more vital to the success of a painting. It is therefore a more important factor to consider when deciding what to paint. Tone, often referred to as value, is the degree of lightness or darkness of a colour. Different colours may have the same tone and one colour may have many different tones. Light or the lack of it determines the tone.

In vision tonal variation enables us to distinguish one object from another and to discern and recognize form. Its relative values permit us to judge distance and perceive space. On the flat picture surface we use tone to give the illusion of these elements; in other words, to suggest three dimensions and to create space.

TONING UP

An interesting play of tones across any view, be it a still-life group, a broad scene or a small detail, makes it a possible subject for a painter. To see tone more clearly look through half-closed eyes. By removing some of the distracting colour it is easier to differentiate between tones. Shapes of a similar tone merge together, while areas of different tones stand out from each other. If a painting works well tonally it it is likely to 'work' overall.

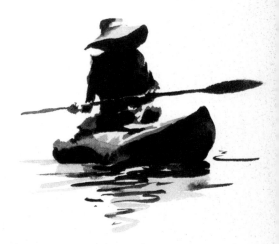

" *The first two things to study are form and values.* "

COROT

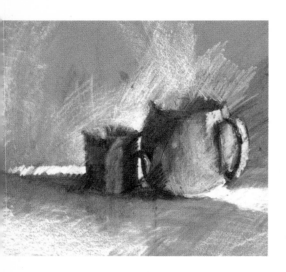

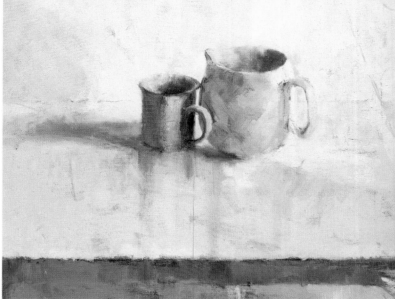

STRONG AND SUBTLE

Amongst any group of items or figures there will be a play of tones. Sometimes these are blatant, sometimes subtle. Strong tonal difference is easy to see, but tiny nuances present just as much pleasure to the artist. Only by trying to record them in paint do you realize just how captivating the differences can be.

Flower heads of one colour and plain-coloured twisting leaves or the folds of plain fabric are great subjects to practise with. Let the natural irregularities of mixed paint or unevenly drying washes play their part also in creating tonal variation.

TUNING IN

When you are observing tone start with comparisons. Ask yourself, 'Is this colour darker or lighter than the one next to it?'. Try to paint the correct relative tones on your paper or board. Remember that the tones of spaces between elements are as important as the tones playing across items themselves and any area of tone may not be limited to a material form; for example, it may include a shadow.

Look for the lightest areas and the darkest areas in the view first. All the other tones will fall in between these two. Comparing colours with a piece of black or white card will help you assess how dark any tone is in relation to black, or how light in relation to white. Sometimes it is hard to decide which tone is the darker between two, especially with very different colours, so keep half-closing your eyes to help you decide.

Small variations in tonal juxtapositions bring a painting alive, literally because they make it real to our eyes. Strengthening tonal differences clarifies a muddled painting because it enables us to read the picture surface.

LIGHT AND CONTRAST

Light is crucial to the artist. Its changing countenance is a great inspiration and dramatic light effects are the subject of many paintings. The subject could be the shaft of light through a

ABOVE LEFT: **Spilling Light**
56 x 71 cm (22 x 28 in), conté crayon
On a piece of mid-tone paper I only needed white and black conté crayon to study the tonal values of this mug and jug. The sweep of the conté crayon strokes indicates the sense of light entering and spilling out of the two items.

ABOVE: **Mug and Jug**
61 x 76 cm (24 x 30 in), oil on canvas
Using the same subject I chose just two colours – Yellow Ochre and French Ultramarine – plus black and white, to explore the tonal variations in paint. Painting with just a few colours enables you to concentrate on tonal differences more easily.

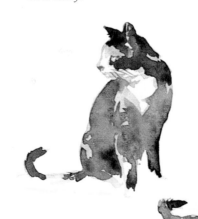

window or a strongly lit still life. Whatever it is, a wide range between the darkest tone and the lightest tone in a painting adds strength and drama to the picture. This distribution of light and shade across the painting is called chiaroscuro.

If a group of objects you have chosen to paint lack fascination place a light source almost directly behind them. View the subject into the light, contre-jour, and against a dark background. The light will escape around the edges of the objects, making an interesting composition of contrasting small lights against rich dark tones.

DAYLIGHT

In the landscape move your position to take advantage of the most favourable light source. Light falling on either side or from behind the subject, rather than lighting directly from the front, will make a more lively play of tones. The low angle of early morning or evening light also creates a more interesting light than the overhead light at midday.

Bussing Home
18 x 13 cm (7 x 5 in), oil on canvas
Painting into the light makes an interesting image as shapes turn into silhouette and small areas of light break out like haloes around dark features.

BELOW: **Study of a Cat**
13 x 18 cm (5 x 7 in), watercolour
In these tonal studies the touch of colour is used as the mid tone. It also adds to the cat's identity.

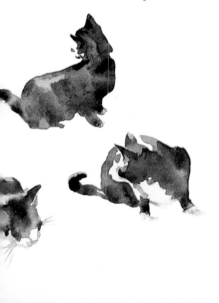

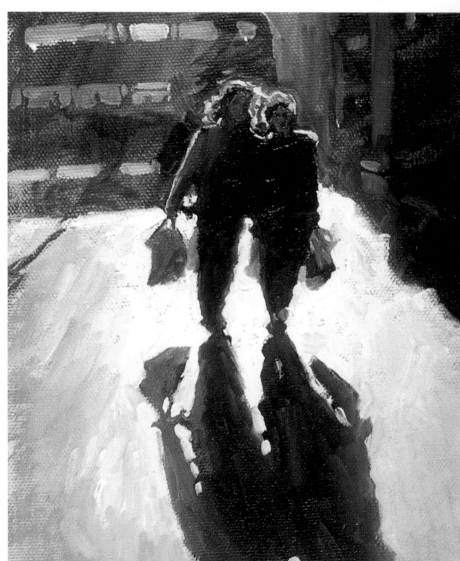

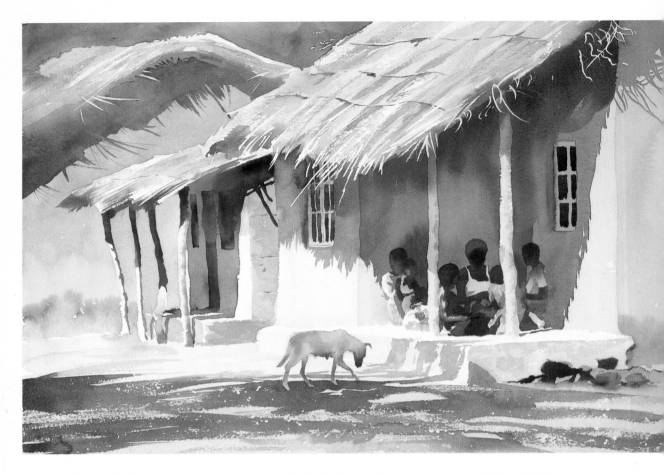

As you look at items or views imagine the light being drawn into them, flowing over them, or spilling out of them. When you paint translate this energy into the painting by the gesture or direction of the brushstroke.

HIGHLIGHTS AND SHADOWS

The bright light of a sunny day often bleaches out the colour of objects it strikes, and throws other areas into a unified darkness, thus simplifying the view into a few main tones. In watercolour the use of the untouched white paper to represent the highlights is a powerful technique. In oils brush or palette-knife strokes of pure or tinted white bring these areas alive.

Shadows nearly always carry a colour either tending to the opposite of the colour of the light source or tinted by reflected colour similar to the light. However dark or light the shadows appear you can vary their strength to suit the painting. All tone is relative, so they can be strengthened or diluted to suit the mood you wish to create.

LACK OF VARIATION

Sometimes there is very little difference in tone across a view. This may in itself be interesting, but most pictures need some contrast of tone. By changing your viewpoint you may be able to find a better composition from the same subject, perhaps by bringing

Telling Stories
43 x 66 cm (17 x 26 in), watercolour
Bathed in shadow under the thatch, the features of the group of people become indistinguishable. This simplification is a gift for the artist, especially in watercolour where you can use wet-in-wet technique to blend colours in a suggestive way.

Opposite: **Holiday Reading**
20 x 25 cm (8 x 10 in), watercolour
The light colours and delicate tints of this watercolour create the cheerful holiday mood enjoyed in this painting of a sunlit table. Imagine this in dark colours; how different the mood would be.

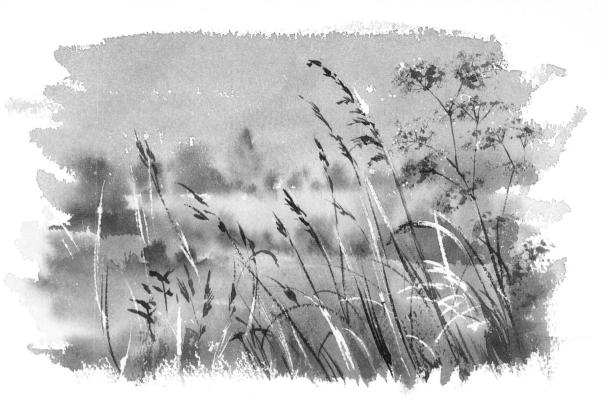

ABOVE: **The Grass Veil**

18 x 25 cm (7 x 10 in), watercolour
The distant fields merged together
in similar tones. To find something
to vary the tone I ducked down,
lowering my eye level, so that the
foreground grasses protruded above
the horizon. The grasses are both
darker and lighter in tone than the
view beyond, creating the variation
needed for interest.

something from the foreground across the view. The proximity of the foreground feature will be a darker or lighter tone than the background and so provide the tonal contrast.

THE TENOR OF TONE

Like colour, tonal values can create specific moods and atmospheres. Light colours tend towards cheerfulness and bright colours are upbeat, whereas dark colours imply gravitas and sobriety. Paintings in a higher key, with lighter colours, feel more lightweight than paintings using a lower key. This does not mean dark paintings are more significant or depressing, nor light paintings frivolous or happy, but it does give you the power to create an overall mood with a predominant tone and to look for that mood in the subject.

You can also use tone to enhance colour. A sallow colour makes the colour beside it appear more lively, and pallid colours make those adjacent more cheerful and bright. In looking at any view isolate small areas from the predominant tone and colour; alone they may sing out and demand to be painted. Do not be afraid of painting very dark washes, or of laying very rich colour as a first wash.

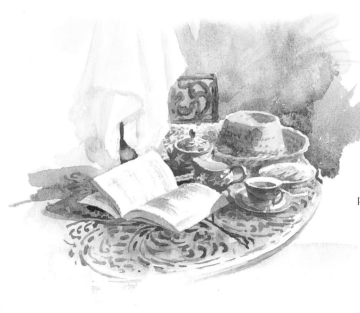

OVER TO YOU...

One of the most effective ways of learning about tonal values is to paint in monochrome. Without the distraction of colour you can concentrate on the differing tones. The resulting studies can also be very striking. For these projects I have chosen to work in watercolour, but feel free to use oils or acrylics if you prefer.

Motto
Light against dark, dark against light.

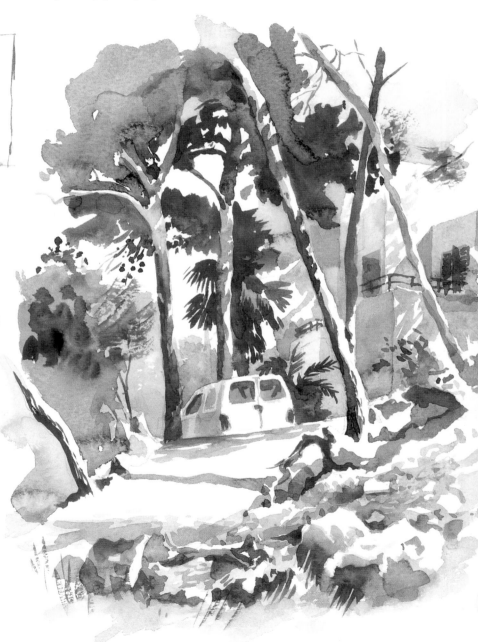

OBSERVING TONAL VARIATION
watercolour
Go outside, taking with you one dark colour. I took Indigo. Half close your eyes on any scene with a play of dark and light shades and paint it with your single colour. Focus all your attention on the variation between the tones and ignore the local colours of the subject.

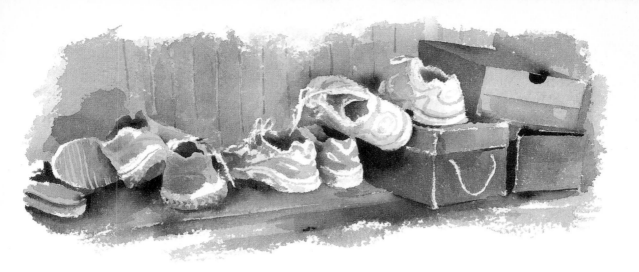

CREATING FORM WITH RELATIVE TONES

watercolour

*Select any pile of clutter or group of objects on a table, shelf or floor.
Do not arrange them. I chose my son's untidy shoes on a shelf. Again,
using just one colour — I used Sepia — create the three-dimensional forms
of the objects chosen. Leave white paper for the lightest areas and note
the darkest darks from the outset. Try to see areas of similar
tone, so that the objects become linked.*

STUDYING SHAPES
IN MONOCHROME

watercolour ink
*Now it gets harder!
This time choose a
moving subject, a figure
or an animal. Use black
watercolour ink, as I have, and a size 3
brush. Constantly dilute and reload the
brush to explore the whole range of tones
from the lightest to the darkest, using
the body of the brush to paint in
shapes rather than line.*

POSTSCRIPT

When you started did you think those subjects would make
good paintings? By the end, did you find them interesting?
(If the answer is 'no', go back to the beginning of the book!)

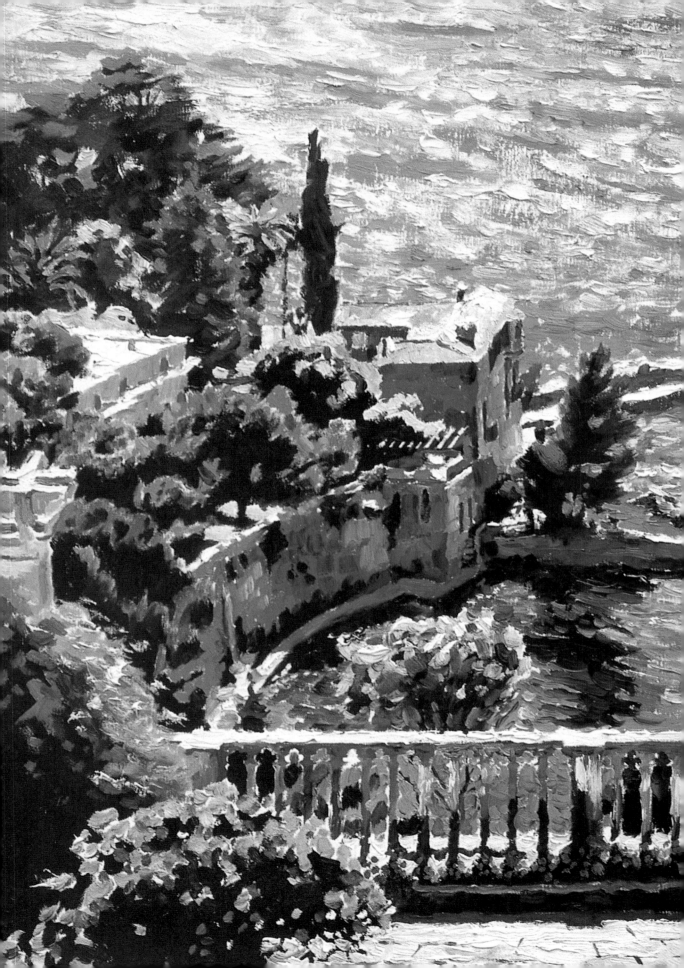

chapter 6

TOUCHING ON TEXTURE

Up to now you have seen that subjects make interesting paintings because of certain combinations of composition, colour and tone. Once the basic requirements of the picture plane are met you can think about the surface texture of the painting, how the paint is laid and the techniques to use; in short, the finished 'look'. Since texture is part of the process of painting it follows that it will also be a rich source of subject matter. Many exciting paintings may originate from the textural qualities of the objects we see, the interesting surfaces of natural and man-made items.

THE PAINTED SURFACE

There is something truly satisfying in portraying texture on the painted surface. Whether it is diligently copied or created by textural painting effects, the results bring pleasure to both painter and viewer.

   The physical consistency of oil paint and acrylics can be used in a literal or suggestive way and watercolour, the flattest of mediums, has a wealth of textural techniques such as dry brush, sponges, wax resist, granulation and salt crystals to create textural illusion.

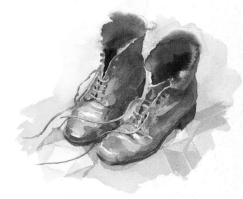

...the surface...should transmit to the beholder the sensation which possessed the artist.

SISLEY

OPPOSITE: **Rothschild Garden,** *51 x 41 cm (20 x 16 in), oil on canvas*

THE INFLUENCE OF TIME

Fascinating textures are found within bark, rocks, seashores and other natural features. Doors and windows with peeling paint and stone and wood grain weathered by the elements make good subject matter. Have the courage to take a small area and indulge in a simple composition.

The wrinkles and lines of an elderly face and close-up portraits carry a strange weight in any medium, while the hunched figures of old age can portray both wisdom and despair.

To emulate the faded colours of decaying opulence mix complementaries with your colours to dull them a little, and work with a very limited palette to avoid over-coloration.

FABRIC TEXTURES

Different fabrics with their range of textures and surfaces offer unlimited choice to the artist. The lacy collars painted by Van

Peeling Paint

*18 x 25 cm (7 x 10 in), watercolour
To appreciate textures of details in the landscape it is necessary either to zoom in on them as in this little painting of the back of an old cart, or to use them as close-up features in the foreground. Here, dry brush and a contrast of tones have been used to create the effects of weathering on painted wood.*

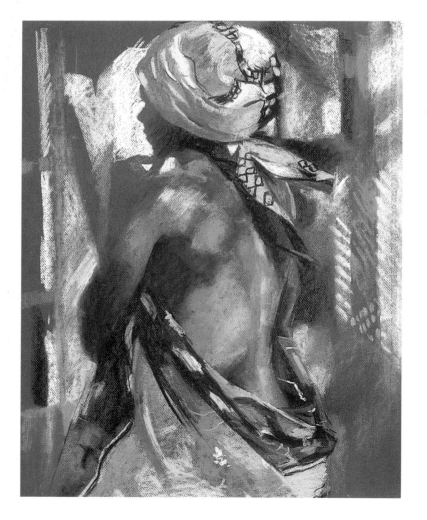

Fabric of Africa

*71 x 51 cm (28 x 20 in), pastel on paper
You can use pattern to help describe form. In this pastel painting the pattern of the sarong, constantly disturbed by folds, is used to show the direction the fabric is taking around the body.*

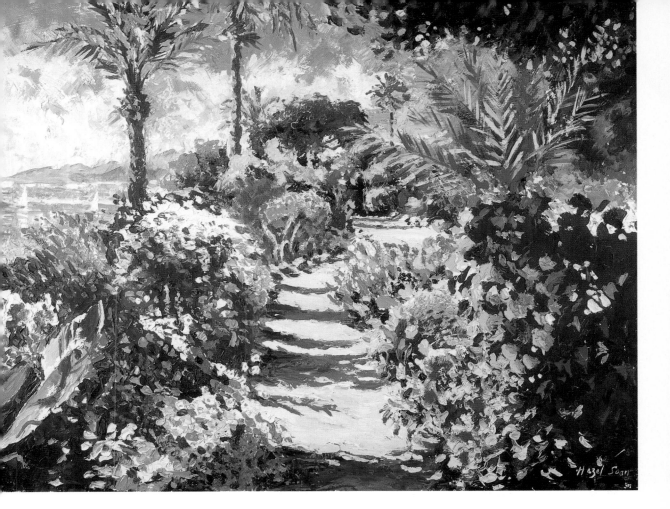

Estepona Pathway

51 x 71 cm (20 x 28 in), oil on paper
*To evoke the abundance of colour
and growth along this Spanish
coastal path the paint is laid in
thick daubs with a palette knife.
The actual surface texture of the
painting becomes as lively as the
experience of seeing.*

Dyck and the ethereal organdies of Klimt have brought ceaseless pleasure to the beholder. To utilize the textures of fabrics in paintings try placing them in conjunction with contrasting items. For example, use them as backdrops or tablecloths in simple still lifes. Remember the picture plane likes pattern and repetition, and the flow lines of drapery can be used to bring the eye into a painting, or lead it out.

Before you paint the surface detail, check that the rise and fall of the form of the fabric works effectively in tonal terms.

FOLIAGE

The patina made by leaves and trees is an ever-changing, ever-painted texture. Avoid the temptation to portray foliage as a collection of meaningless daubs, but seek instead the main shapes and masses in the trees, bushes or shrubs, so that the foliage works as forms first.

The whole surface of the painting can be textured or you can suggest texture in a few areas only. Contrast areas of activity with areas of peace. To imply there is abundant texture with a few hints is often more effective than describing every last leaf and twig.

First impressions are usually the liveliest. Beware overworking your painting. Freshness cannot survive a belated search for unnecessary detail.

OVER TO YOU...

Rocks and stones provide endless fascination when it comes to exploring texture. Since the forms are irregular no-one can tell you their shape is wrong. Once you have established the solidity of the stones with tone you can have fun with their surfaces. Try out some of the techniques on these pages and apply them to other subjects too.

Motto
Do not fiddle.

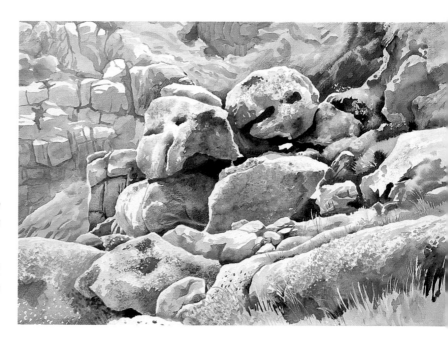

▶ SPONGING

56 x 76 cm (22 x 30 in), watercolour
Using a natural sponge to press the watercolour onto the paper paints a wonderful, slightly random, mottled patina perfect for granite rocks. Mix plenty of creamy liquid paint before you start as the sponge will absorb the paint rapidly from the pool in the palette.

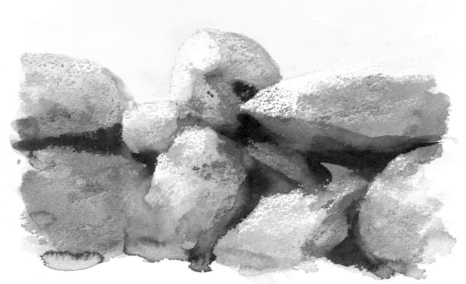

◀ WAX RESIST

watercolour
White candle wax is rubbed over the highlit surfaces of the stones before painting. Where the wax repels the watercolour an uneven grainy texture is created. The wax can be rubbed over layers of dried watercolour and painted with successive washes to bring texture into the dark areas.

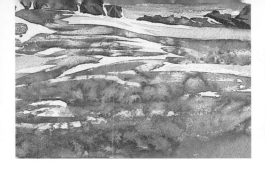

▲ SALT CRYSTALS (detail)

watercolour

If you drop salt crystals into pools of paint the absorption of the pigment by the crystals creates exquisite circular and star-shaped patterns that are similar to the patterns of lichen on rocks. The paint takes a long time to dry, so be careful not to brush the salt off too soon.

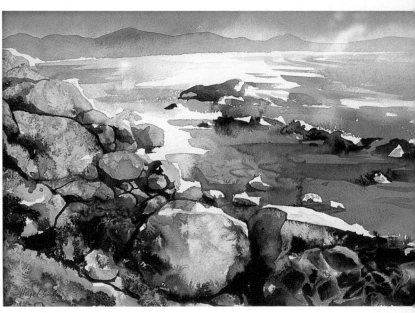

▲ CLINGFILM

28 x 36 cm (11 x 14 in), watercolour

The texture in this painting is produced by laying clingfilm over the wet paint and lifting it off when dry. I find there is little control over the results, so be prepared for a few disasters among your successes!

◄ BRUSHWORK (detail)

oil on board

The consistency of oil paint creates texture by default even when painted with small brushes. The colours of the lichen are dragged over the surface with undiluted paint so that the strands of the brush leave texture in their wake.

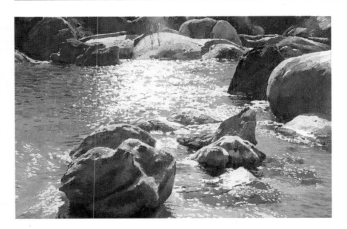

◄ PHYSICAL TEXTURE

76 x 102 cm (30 x 40 in), oil on canvas

The sparkly water among the rocks has a prominent texture. A palette knife is used to apply white paint in clean daubs for the light on the water, and smeared and scraped over the rocks.

POSTSCRIPT

When you have had a go, re-read Sisley's words at the beginning of the chapter. Have you achieved this?

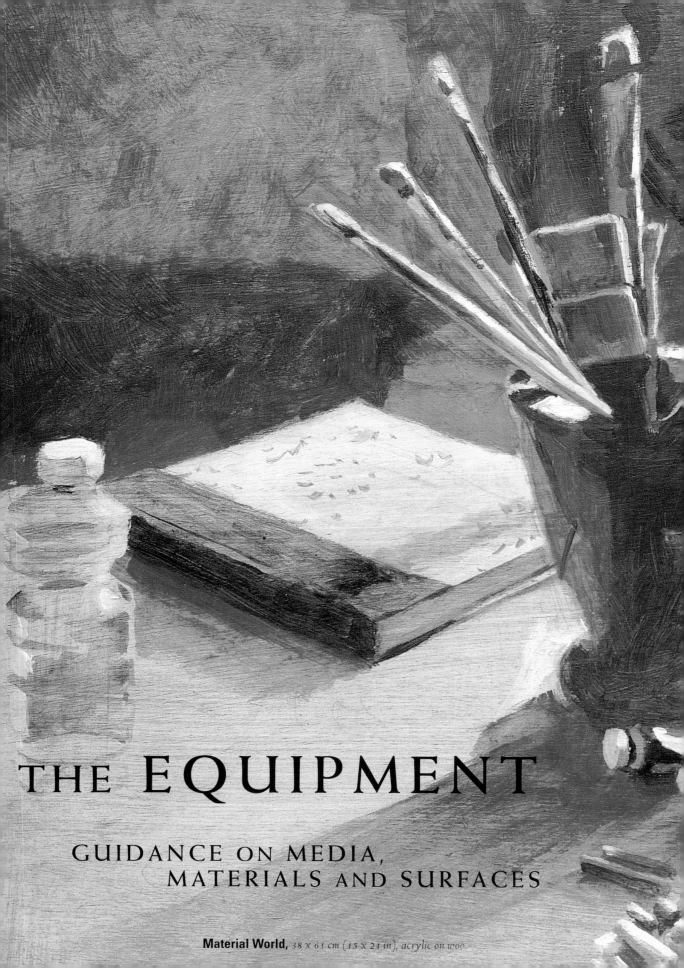

THE EQUIPMENT

GUIDANCE ON MEDIA, MATERIALS AND SURFACES

Material World, *38 x 61 cm (15 x 24 in), acrylic on woo*

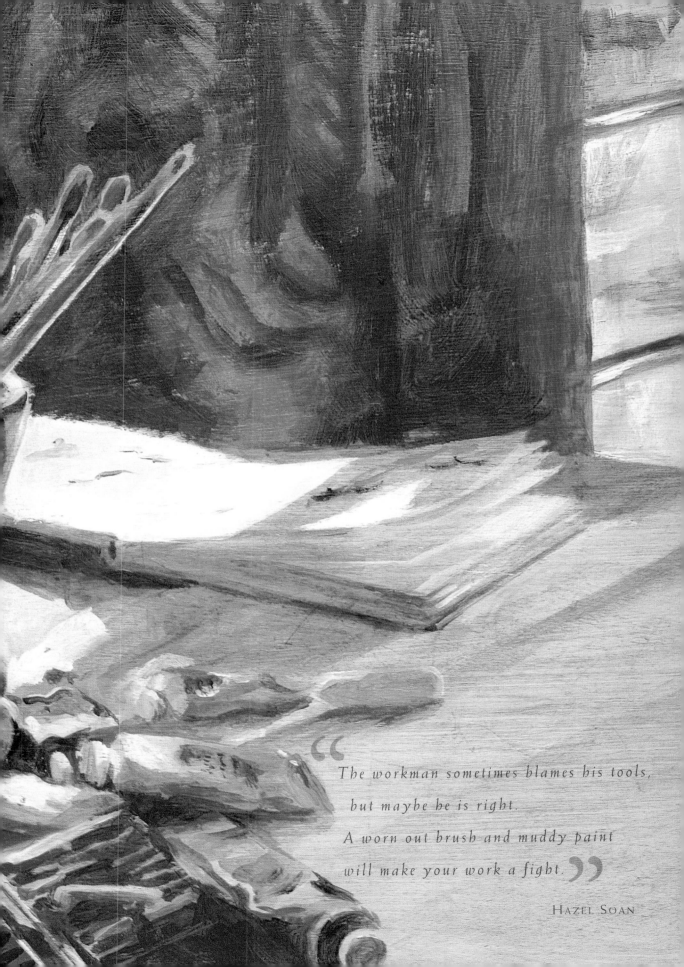

The workman sometimes blames his tools,
   but maybe he is right.
A worn out brush and muddy paint
will make your work a fight.

HAZEL SOAN

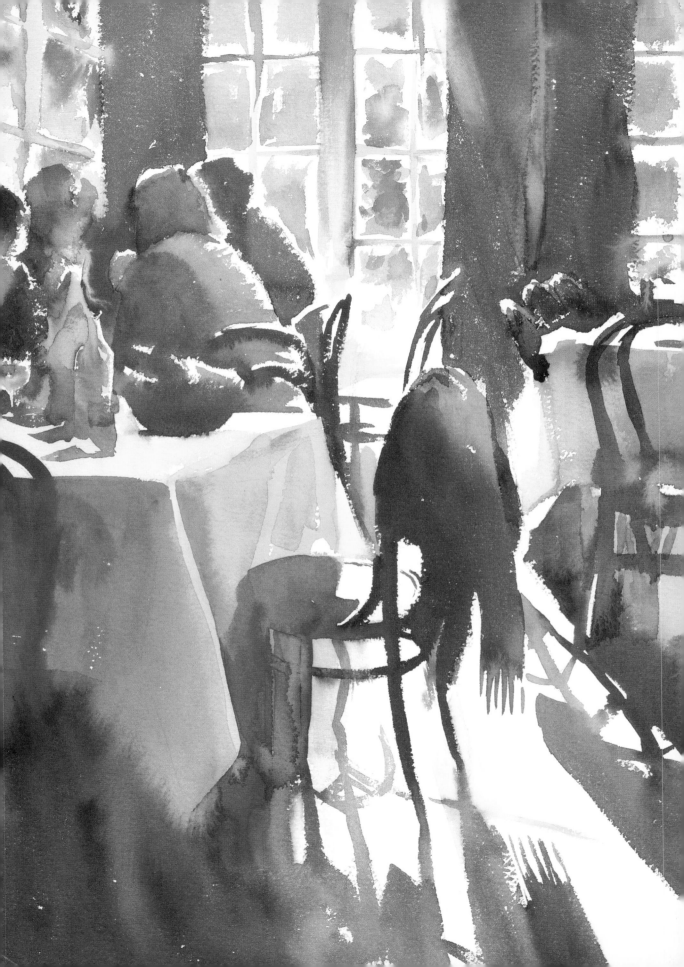

chapter 7

TOOLS OF THE TRADE

This section is more a checklist on materials and techniques than a list of requirements. It assumes you already own some painting equipment and suggests tools and surfaces and ways to employ them that might expand your repertoire.

Painters do not need vast amounts of equipment. Over time you will gather more brushes and paint, but usually find, as with most things in life, that the items you use most often are actually quite few.

WELL EQUIPPED

Sometimes the very tools chosen to further your painting are actually holding you back. It is said that bad workmen always blame their tools rather than themselves, but you cannot cut a clean edge with a blunt saw. Too often I see amateur artists struggling to make paintings with cheap or worn brushes. Others battle to choose from a palette of far too many colours, or mix watercolours on plastic palettes that resist water. There is no point setting out on an adventure improperly equipped, so now that we have honed the eye let us check out the practical elements needed on this exciting visual journey.

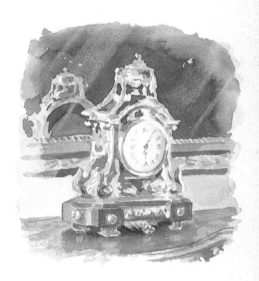

" *In art intentions are not sufficient...* "

PICASSO

OPPOSITE: **Among Friends,** *53 x 36 cm (21 x 14 in), watercolour*

WATERCOLOUR PAINTS AND BRUSHES

I often find people reach better results mixing watercolour paint from tubes than from pans, especially if they require large amounts of colour. Another benefit is that it prevents you using too many colours in one painting, which is easily done if the colours are inviting you from the palette! I tend to take my reds and yellows from pans and use tubes for the colours I use in abundance.

Many aspiring watercolourists work with brushes that are too small for the painting. Maybe they think this gives them more control, but this is not true. Any round, pure sable brush, size 7–12, with a good tip, can achieve broad brushstrokes for washes and fine lines for details. Fiddling around with small brushes denies the watercolour its liveliness and encourages needless overpainting.

The success of watercolour painting lies in knowing how much water to use with the pigment. No one can teach you this; it is gleaned through practice alone.

ACRYLIC AND OIL PAINTS

In consistency oils and acrylics are similar, but acrylics have the added advantage of drying quickly and enabling you to over paint in the same session. You can also use acrylics like watercolours, building up your painting in overlaying glazes and with swift-drying transparent colours.

Limited Palette, Unlimited Colour

28 x 36 cm (11 x 14 in), watercolour
In watercolour painting you need very few colours, and the less you use the more your painting will hold together. This sketch uses just three colours – Cadmium Red, Cobalt Blue and Cadmium Yellow. These, and just one Rowney size 9 sable brush, create all the colours of the palette.

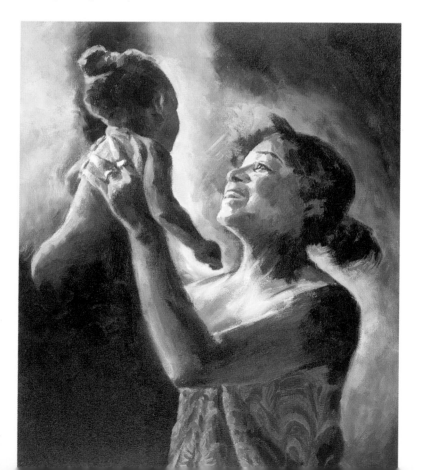

Joie de Vie

76 x 61 cm (30 x 24 in), acrylic on canvas
Paint does not have to be applied evenly all over the surface to create a finished painting; there can be areas of thinly stained canvas and areas of thickly applied paint. The same three colours with the addition of white are used here as in the watercolour above.

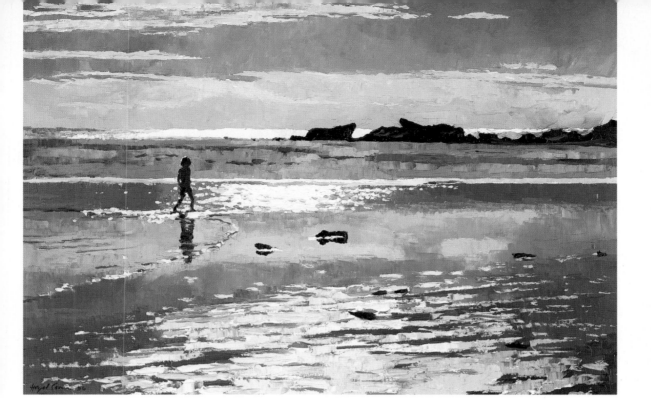

Dreaming

56 x 76 cm (22 x 30 in), oil laid with palette knife on canvas
To avoid muddy turpentine altogether try using a palette knife. Broad flat washes can be scraped on and off, patches of paint laid and even small details are possible. To clean, simply wipe the knife with a rag!

The gesture of the brushstroke in oils and acrylics creates lively brushmarks. As the sticky brushstrokes blend into each other the irregularity of the mixing colours makes exciting blends. The less control exerted over this the more life the painting tends to have.

The most common problem faced in oils is muddiness. This is partly due to their opaque nature, partly due to using dirty turpentine and mostly due to too much adjusting of colours while they are still wet on the canvas.

Clean paint is dependent on deciding on the colour and mixing the pigments on the palette before applying them to the canvas. To keep this freshness in your painting you need to use several different brushes at a time and rinse any brushes in turpentine from a continually refreshed jar.

ADDITIONAL MEDIA AND TOOLS

The stickiness of oils and acrylics enables you to mix textures into the paint before it dries. Sand or powdered pigment is particularly good for real texture and marble dust for luminescence. Nowadays there are also plenty of tubs for sale with readymade gels and stucco that can be added to the paint.

Any media can be applied with natural sponges. Paint can be dripped from containers, flicked from brushes, spattered from toothbrushes, rinsed off with a tap or rubbed off with a rag to make different textures or effect corrections. Adding pen and black ink to watercolour has a graphic quality and strengthens a weak picture. Coloured inks contribute vibrant and rich textures to the painted image and pastel laid over weak transparent washes of watercolour restores vibrancy. Texture can be scraped or pressed into all media with knives, combs, fabrics and other tools.

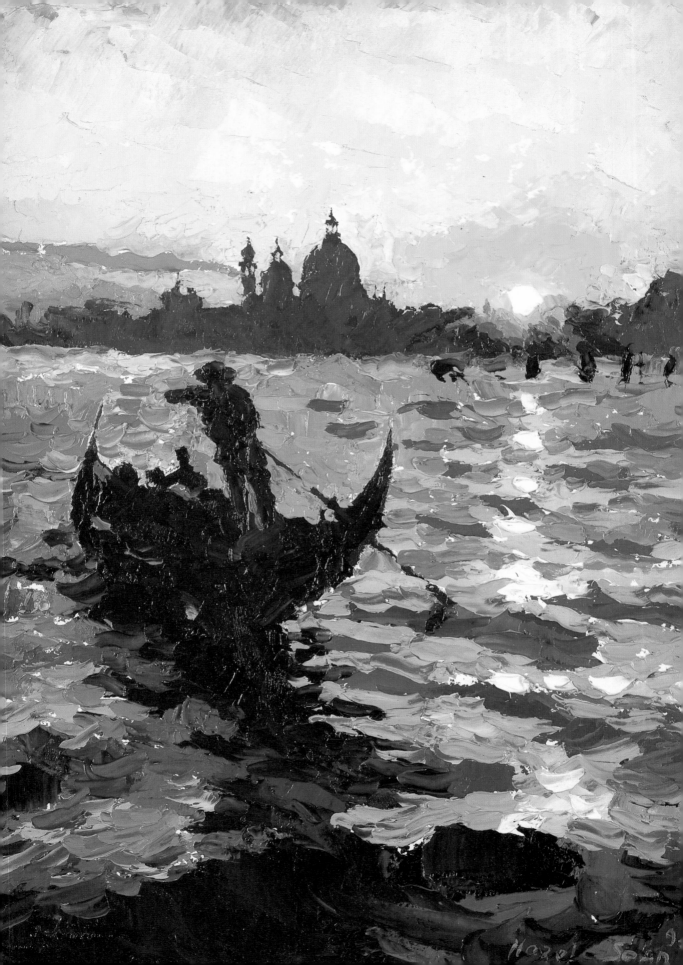

chapter 8

THE PICTURE PLANE

Some subjects seem to demand certain surfaces, sizes and shapes and as the ground will also determine the look of the painting it may in turn influence the subject you choose to paint. Deciding the proportion of your picture surface is a prerequisite for composition. It will influence the way you see your subject and what you choose to include in your painting.

Paper is a universal ground. It comes in many thicknesses and textures and can be used for watercolour, acrylic and, if primed, oils too. It can easily be cut to any proportion at any stage in the painting.

WATERCOLOUR ON PAPER

Watercolour causes thin papers to buckle, so it is necessary either to stretch the paper prior to use or to tape it down securely on all sides. Heavy papers, however, do not buckle from wet washes and the thickest – 640 gsm (300 lb) or more – do not require stretching whatever size you paint. For outside work sketchblocks in which the paper is stuck down at the edges to prevent buckling are really useful as the page cannot be blown by the wind.

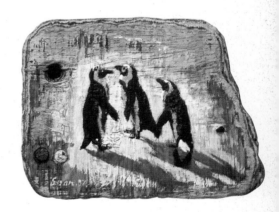

I like painting on a square because you don't have to decide whether it should be longer or shorter...

WARHOL

OPPOSITE: **The Gondola,** 28 x 20 cm (11 x 8 in), oil on 640 gsm (300 lb) paper

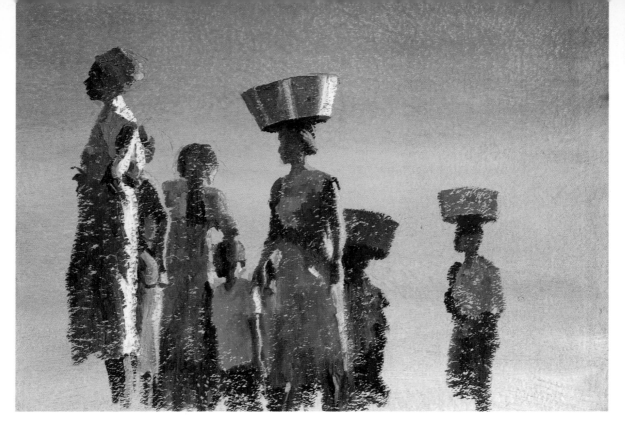

OILS AND ACRYLICS ON PAPER

The oil from oil paint will seep out into unprimed paper and probably rot it with time. An acrylic primer over the paper or a couple of thin washes of acrylic paint will prevent this and make a lovely smooth, slightly textured surface to paint on. The paint dries quicker on paper than on canvas.

Acrylics, being plastic, and mixed with water, can be painted straight onto paper, but if you wish to avoid the paint being absorbed by the paper prime it first with a thin wash of acrylic paint, acrylic primer or emulsion paint. You can also create a coloured ground in this way.

TINTED PAPERS

As a watercolourist you are not limited to white paper. The radiance of the transparent colours may be at its richest on a white ground, but it looks equally lovely on tinted papers, or over white paper tinted with a coloured wash. With the addition of opaque white watercolour or gouache you can use still darker grounds. I love to utilize the buff-coloured cardboard at the back of the sketchbook, or paint on brown wrapping paper.

Nowadays there is a vast array of hand-made papers with numerous textures and interesting tints. Experiment on these and you may find some suit you better than others. Heavy texture will certainly challenge the way you lay paint.

If you find yourself without paper turn to the back of hotel bills, old newspapers, brochures and disposable menus.

The Catch

46 x 56 cm (18 x 22 in),
oil on handmade paper
This highly textured paper was primed with pale blue acrylic paint. The surface became a lovely mid-tone ground to paint on with oils, and the increased weight of the paper gave it substance.

The Tote

5 x 10 cm (2 x 4 in),
watercolour on betting ticket
Losing on the horses need not be so bad! Having no sketchbook to hand, this betting ticket proved a perfect compromise.

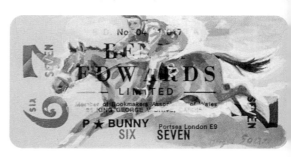

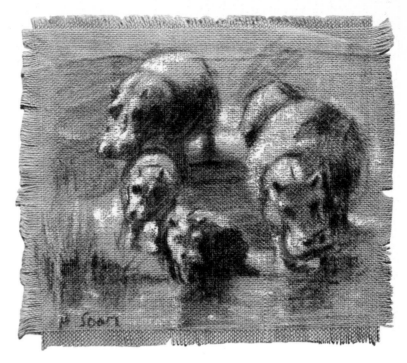

Mud, Glorious Mud
41 x 43 cm (16 x 17 in), oil on hessian
Black and white oil paint on
unprimed and frayed hessian create
an entertaining picture of hippos
coming down to water.

Painting Miniatures
25 x 18 cm (10 x 7 in),
watercolour and gouache on black card
Deep black mounting board was
the perfect ground to bring out the
luminosity of night-time luxuries.

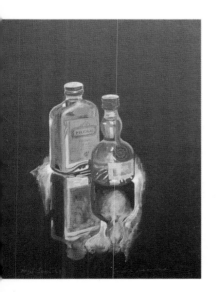

CANVAS

The flexible size and textures of canvas make it a favoured surface for oils and acrylics. Canvas is highly absorbent and ideally should be sized and primed before painting with oils. However, if you wish to paint with stains of oil colour and want the colour to run and blend in the fabric only a light sizing is preferable. Acrylics will not rot canvas, so you can use it unprimed, and staining with these is safer fume wise!

OTHER GROUNDS

Oils were first painted on wood, then canvas. Wood is a lovely surface to paint on, having grain and being rigid. Wood on a large scale is very heavy and solid wood is expensive, but marine ply is a lighter non-bowing alternative and provides a good unyielding surface on which to paint. Oils and acrylics adhere to most surfaces; you can paint on hardboard, plaster, walls, stones, driftwood or fabrics.

I also enjoy painting oils on the backing boards of sketchbooks. A ground tinted with a mid tone frees you from the fear and frustration of covering all that blank canvas with something, which is an onerous task in a large painting. If, however, the mid tones are already in place, painting the darks and adding the highlights at the outset will quickly give you the essence of the painting.

You can tint the ground yourself; earth colours make an excellent base, but you can work on reds, blues, siennas, greys, or any other colour and achieve exciting results.

Take inspiration from the Bloomsbury artists: Vanessa Bell and Duncan Grant painted on surfaces all over their home at Charleston, in Sussex, creating a unique environment.

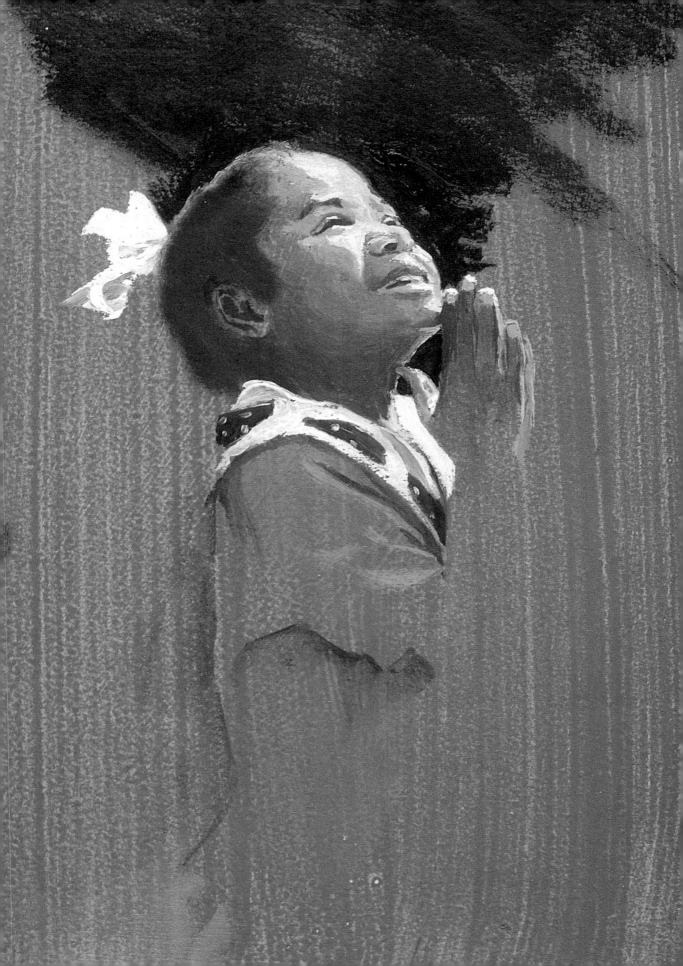

chapter 9

AN APPROPRIATE
MEDIUM

The vast array of materials open to the painter today makes choosing the right medium for a painting very exciting, but also more difficult. Any subject can be painted with any medium, and different media, with their diverse applications, require a different approach to the subject, influencing the subject choice.

Neither should limitation of means be considered a disadvantage; improvisation stretches the creative muscles and engenders new ideas.

FITTING THE PURPOSE

Sometimes paintings are simply records of our visual world or the response to visual stimuli. At other times we are deeply touched and want to convey to others the sincerity of that emotion. Imagination in art lies in finding the most complete expression. Choosing the right conveyance is as important as seeing the shapes, colours and tones that make something into a painting.

There are no rules about medium preference. Practice and personal choice will in the end dictate. Follow your inclinations and you will find your own milieu.

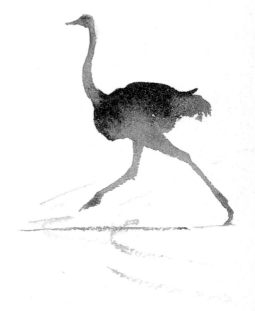

> *The artist does not draw what he sees,*
> *but what he must make others see.*
>
> DEGAS

OPPOSITE: **Give Us This Day,** *30 x 23 cm (12 x 9 in), oil on paper*

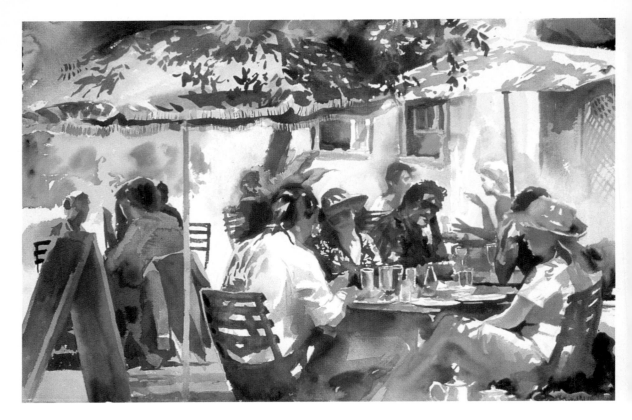

CHOOSING A MEDIUM

Speed of application can determine your choice. Watercolours can be swiftly painted and can quickly render translucent, ethereal subjects, such as skies and moving incidents. They are also light to carry and clean to use, and require easily available water, so they are ideal for the travelling artist or for someone with limited space to work. If you are seeking speed, radiance and spontaneity watercolours would be a good choice; they are fast for the busy, kind to the cautious and thrilling for the free.

When it comes to texture there is far more versatility with oils and acrylics. In some respects oils and acrylics are more forgiving than watercolour because they can be easily reworked. In opaque media you can work from dark to light, which confers a rich density on the painting. Some subjects require a stronger 'look'; strong contrasts and three-dimensional forms welcome depth.

THE FACTOR OF SCALE

Scale, too, can determine your choice. Paper in very large sizes is unwieldy, so if you choose to work large, canvas, wood or board are the likely surface and will affect the medium you use. Contrasts of light work well in fairly small watercolours, but to paint the same subject on a bigger scale would require so much paint for the dark areas that you would find it easier to use oils.

Because of their opacity and consequent visual strength oil paintings are clearer to appreciate from a distance, whereas the subtle qualities of watercolours welcome closer inspection, especially once they are protected behind glass.

Café, Church Street

43 x 64 cm (17 x 25 in), watercolour
The dancing, radiant sunlight and moving people made watercolour my first choice for this painting. The same subject painted in oils or acrylics could look just as sunny, but it would have a different 'feel' and probably take longer to paint.

Opposite: **The Long Shadows**
25 x 41 cm (10 x 16 in), acrylic on paper
For quick landscapes acrylics are very versatile. Here they have been painted in thin glazes for the sky, trees and field and then used more thickly to build up the grasses in the foreground. Pale opaque yellows have been used to retrieve lights lost in the haste of painting.

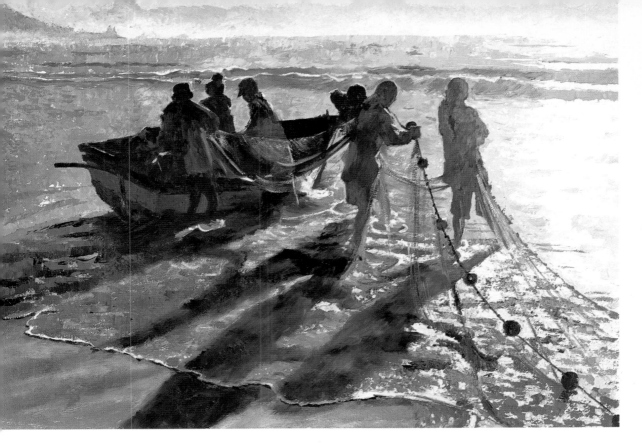

Gather the Dawn

56 x 76 cm (22 x 30 in), oil on paper
I made several small sketches of the
fishermen at dawn in watercolour,
but when it came to painting a
larger piece I could only imagine it
in oils. The strong contrast of
silhouettes with dazzling dawn light
and the time-honoured simplicity
of drawing in the nets somehow
required the opacity of oils.

TRANSPARENCY, GLAZING AND TINTS

As well as mixing colours on the palette, watercolours, oils and acrylics can all be laid in successive tints of transparent colour. Watercolour painting is all about laying coloured tints one over another, but also in acrylics and oils you can enliven a colour by overlaying or glazing that colour with a hue of similar temperature. You can also dull down colours and increase or decrease contrast between adjacent hues by using complementaries. Garish colours can be calmed down simply by overlaying a tint of the complementary colour.

IMPROVISATION

The beauty of painting is that there is nothing you cannot paint, and nothing you cannot paint with. You are not concerned with the longevity of the painting – experiment with any media on any ground. Surprise yourself by working with unfamiliar media. Quite quickly you will find your own preference and scale; you will be irritated with one method and delighted with another.

You are not even limited to conventional pigments and art materials. I have resorted to using coffee in place of Burnt Sienna and have painted on newspapers and bills when no paper is at hand!

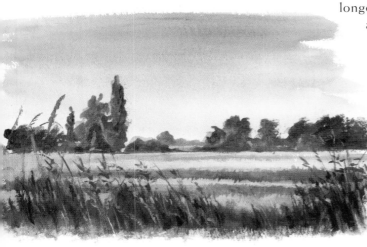

THE ADVENTURE

DISCOVERING SUBJECTS ON LOCATION

Over the Dunes 20 x 30 cm (8 x 12 in), oil on canvas

> " *Your eyes are honed, your vision clear,*
> *your palette primed to go;*
> *the inspiration's everywhere,*
> *a vital world to know.* "
>
> HAZEL SOAN

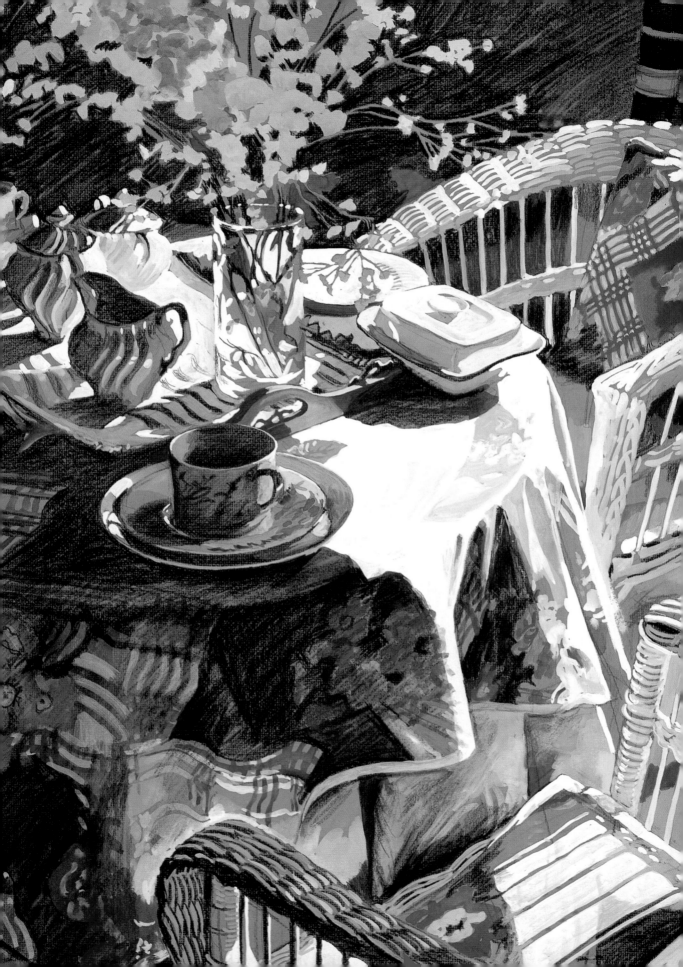

chapter 10

AT HOME

The easiest place to pick up a paintbrush is in the comfort of your own home, out in the garden or in the shelter of a balcony or patio. Still-life, figure and interior subjects abound, and some of the best subjects are the least obvious. Before you clear the table check it out for potential compositions, or instead of moaning at the children for watching too much TV make the most of them sitting still, a perfect pose for a painting! And do not be so quick to clear up the cast-aside shoes; they probably make a great picture too.

BE YOURSELF

There are always the traditional fallbacks such as the vase of flowers, the bowl of fruit, or the composed still life. These all-time favourites make great subjects, but by choosing these you may be missing out on the things that say so much more about your life. Modern Art is often self-confessional, so why not let your painting proclaim the fascination of your everyday life too.

Swift paintings can have just as much integrity as laboured versions. Paintings are made one brush stroke at a time. If each one is enjoyed and loaded with concentration your paintings cannot fail.

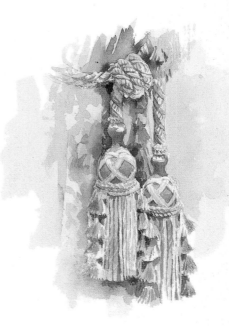

To paint ... paint ... without being afraid of painting badly ...

MONET

OPPOSITE: **East Meets West,** *69 x 51 cm (27 x 20 in), watercolour, gouache and conté crayon on paper*

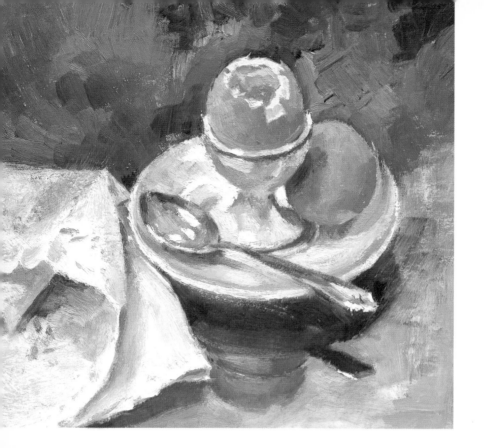

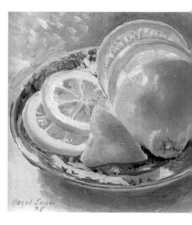

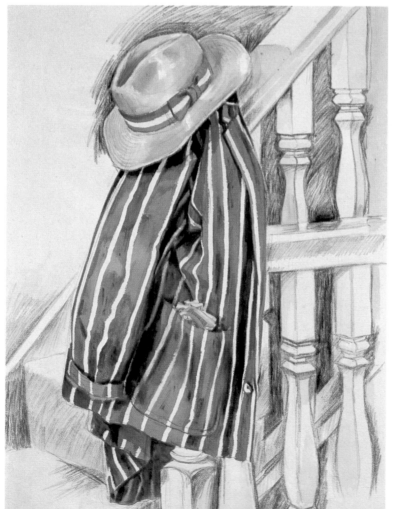

LEFT: **Born with a Silver Spoon**
28 x 28 cm (11 x 11 in), oil on board
Do not clear away the breakfast things before assessing their validity as a subject; in fact, do not even eat your breakfast before making a quick sketch! It does not take long to squeeze onto a palette, French Ultramarine, Yellow Ochre, black and white; and the painting took less than an hour.

ABOVE: **In Advance of a G&T**
15 x 15 cm (6 x 6 in), oil on board
The contrast of colour between the yellow and the blue was the initial attraction here. As I painted I became fascinated with the shadows on the lemon and the odd greeny tinge to the juicy flesh of the lemon.

LEFT: **The Good Life**
91 x 61 cm (36 x 24 in), acrylic and conté crayon on canvas
A discarded blazer and panama hat flung over the newel post might seem an odd subject, but when the stripes of the jacket echo the banister rail and posts and a canvas is at hand a potential painting is born. I worked in acrylic for speed in case the owner returned to claim my subject!

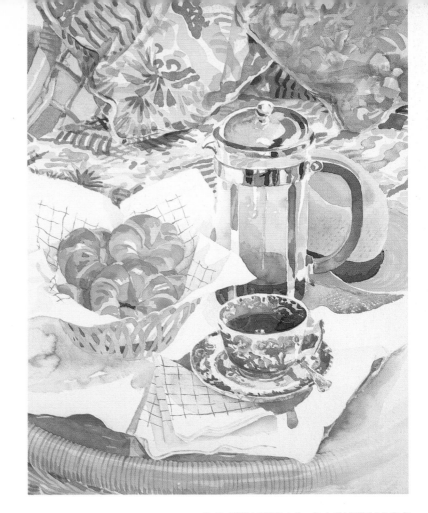

Coffee and Croissants

56 x 38 cm (22 x 15 in), watercolour
The freshness of leaving white paper in watercolour for the whites is used to good effect for the crisp serviettes and the shine on the cafetière. Yellow Ochre, French Ultramarine, Alizarin Crimson and Cadmium Red are the only colours used.

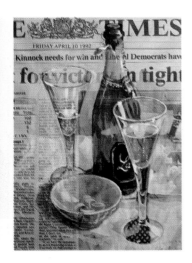

Cause for Celebration

30 x 23 cm (12 x 9 in), watercolour and white gouache on newspaper
Watercolour is the perfect medium for the spur-of-the-minute painting. Carry a small palette and brush in your pocket and any paper will do as a surface.

POTENTIAL PAINTINGS

Look around, just sitting where you are. Remember all the things a good painting needs – interesting shapes, contrasting colours, differing tones. Half close your eyes; a play of tones is easier to see once colour is excluded. Home in on the smallest detail, such as the corner of a newspaper, a cup, or the light on a bottle or glass. If you cannot find anything to excite you widen your view a little, and move your vision left and right, up and down.

INTERESTING THINGS

The joy of painting objects that sit still is the chance to really look at all the little innuendos of tone and colour and interpret them in paint. Overlapping objects in the composition makes it easier to suggest space. Try to paint with the whole picture in mind to avoid leaving isolated items. You do not have to be too ambitious; a fragment painted well is better than a whole picture painted badly. The painting does not even have to be finished to be interesting.

Light falling from, or seen through, windows is an excellent place to find potential paintings. Table tops and surfaces lit from behind carry a wonderful sheen and offer reflections and deep shadows from their occupants. The details of an object seen against the light will dissolve away when you half close your eyes; remember this when you come to paint.

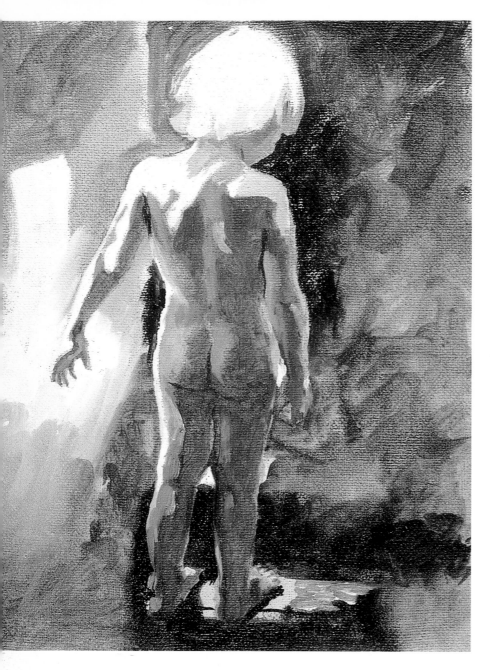

Stepping Out

20 x 15 cm (8 x 6 in), oil on canvas
Children change so fast that any
painting of a moment caught in
time will be treasured later. Back
views are often more telling than
front views as the shape of the
person and their pose identifies their
character without the facial
features demanding attention.

FAMILY AND FRIENDS

At home someone around you will either sit still long enough to give you a chance to paint them, or you will become very good at quick sketches! The essence of movement, even in the still figure, is an important way of breathing life into your figures. Brushstrokes with a dance in their step, blurred passages of colour, even slight inaccuracies in drawing or elongated proportion, all add life to paintings of people. You do not need to overload faces with detail, nor even worry too much about likeness.

If someone is sitting in a chair or lying on a bed, blend their shaded side into the fabric of the support so that they rest in it and are not separate from it.

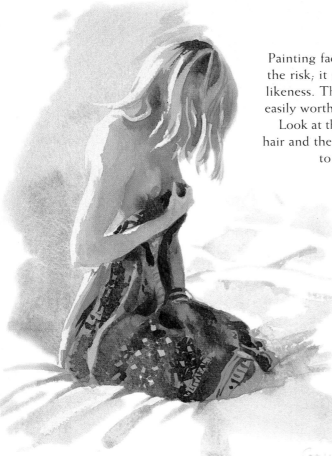

FACES AND FEATURES

Painting faces is always challenging and fascinating. Take the risk; it does not really matter if you cannot catch the likeness. The shared joy of painting and being painted is easily worth the worst of end results.

Look at the proportion and shape of the overall head and hair and the positions of the features of the face in relation to each other. A person's likeness and character are held just as much within these proportions as they are in the actual features themselves.

A portrait does not have to be head on, or head and shoulders. The face can be almost hidden behind hair or hands, or wreathed in darkness. You can paint just the eyes, just the mouth or even the hands on their own. A face can be blown up to enormous proportions, painted with unnatural colours or painted and scraped off to form a blur. There are no rules, even in portraiture.

And there is always the mirror. Here you will be able to paint and draw to your heart's content the most sympathetic model of all!

ABOVE: **The Sarong**
25 x 18 cm (10 x 7 in), watercolour
In this gentle sketch of my sister, Mary, the colour of the sarong is run into the folds of the bed linen to 'sit' the figure into the soft fabric.

Louis and Oopa

13 x 18 cm (5 x 7 in), watercolour
This portrait of grandfather and grandson is painted into the light and simplified into two tones — light and dark. Burnt Sienna was washed over the whole paper and then Sepia and Burnt Sienna mixed together for the dark tone. Even with such simplicity much is said about their relationship.

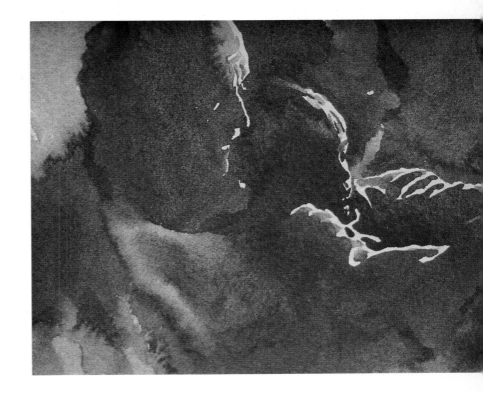

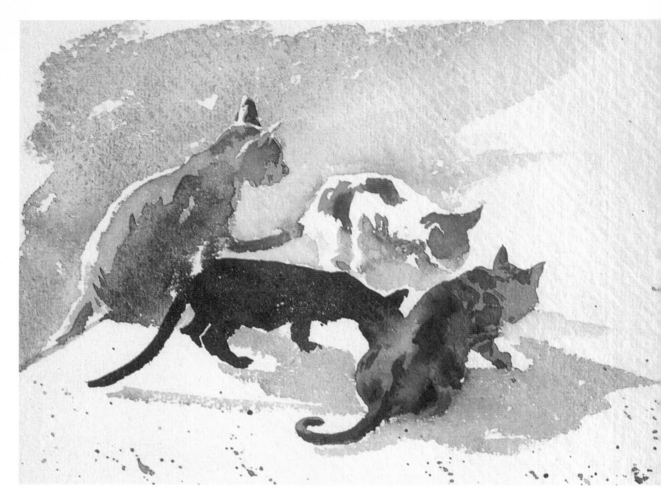

ANIMALS AROUND

Cats and dogs and other beloved pets make wonderful, if not always obliging, subject matter. My favoured medium would be watercolour, where the natural blends of wet-in-wet washes create the patterns of hair and fur almost by default. Take care not to make the animals appear static or stiff.

Charcoal or brush and ink drawings of elegant felines make excellent studies and are a great way to learn how cats move and to see the shapes they make. Swift fluid brushstrokes make it easier to catch the walking motion of dogs than drawing with a pencil. The lovely tangle of legs of resting and sleeping animals is always a joy to paint; note the positions quickly before they roll over and make yet another great pose.

YOUR OWN BACKYARD

Outside in the garden or on the balcony you will find an inexhaustible supply of mini landscapes and still lifes. A single flower or sprig of leaves, a broken branch or cracked flowerpot vie for equal attention with flower borders and leafy bowers. My attention is always drawn to bags of compost, watering cans and broken fences, especially if lit

ABOVE: **Cats on the Scrounge**
13 x 18 cm (5 x 7 in), watercolour
To paint the irregular patterns of fur touch the stripes or patches of colour into wet washes so that the colours merge softly.

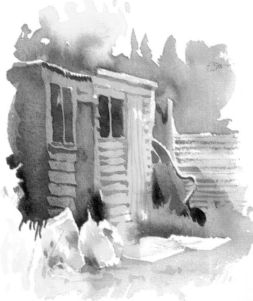

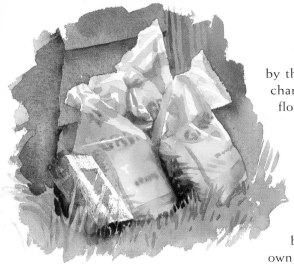

The Gravel Bags

10 x 10 cm (4 x 4 in), watercolour
In any view there is a choice of
composition. In The Potting
Shed *(below left) the wide view is*
shown, but I preferred to zoom in
on the gravel bags. The focal point
was the V-shaped space between
the top halves of the left and right
foreground bags.

RIGHT: **Monday Morning Reds**

30 x 20 cm (12 x 8 in), watercolour
Trust your instincts; telling
someone you have just been
painting the washing on the line
may sound odd to them, but for the
painter there is just as much interest
to be found in the changing colours
of a curling cloth as there is in a
complex interior.

OPPOSITE: **The Potting Shed**

10 x 8 cm (4 x 3 in), watercolour
An untidy corner of the garden can
prove interesting for a quick sketch.
The delicious blends of watercolour
washes almost romanticize this
scruffy subject.

by the sun. Weather-worn discarded items hold as much charm as the abundant lovingly tended displays of flowerpots and window boxes.

Look for tonal interplay, fascinating shapes and interaction of colour. Check that your chosen subject has a focal point, a main point of interest, and give your attention to that area in making the painting.

PRIME TIME

The chief delight of painting at home is the ease it bestows on your painting time. You can work at your own pace, in privacy, without having to lug your materials around. Oils and acrylics become as convenient as watercolour and everything around you has something to do with your life. Take advantage of this, even if you can spare only an hour; it will be an hour well spent, and well rewarded.

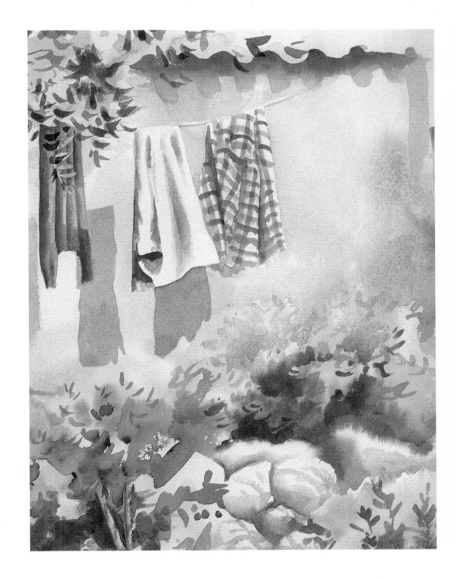

demonstration in oils
GREEN APPLES

COLOURS
Prussian Blue
Titanium White
Rowney Yellow
Indian Yellow
Sap Green
French Ultramarine
Raw Umber
Burnt Sienna

Ordinary items make great subjects. The spherical forms of apples offer shiny highlights on their surfaces and intriguing dark corners where they meet and overlap. Add to that the dominant stripes of a tea towel and the subtle tonal changes on a brown paper bag and you have a satisfying couple of hours' painting ahead of you!

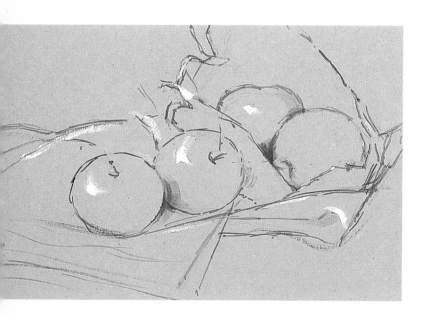

1 I spilled the fruit onto the folded cloth and shifted them slightly until I was happy with the arrangement. I studied the colours and tones and took from my paintbox the colours I wanted. I sketched out the main shapes in relation to each other with dilute Prussian Blue, looking for flow lines and cross referencing all the time. The backing board of a sketchbook is a good surface for oil painting as the buff-grey colour provides a mid tone from the start. I marked in the highlights and dark corners.

2 I followed the flow of the stripes with dark Prussian Blue to create the folded form of the fabric. Then, starting from the middle of the composition, setting one tone and colour against another, I began to paint the apples and paper bag, not as apples and paper but as different tones and colours joining up across the surface of the picture plane. By using a mid-tone ground the three-dimensional forms quickly began to take shape as the lights and darks were emphasized.

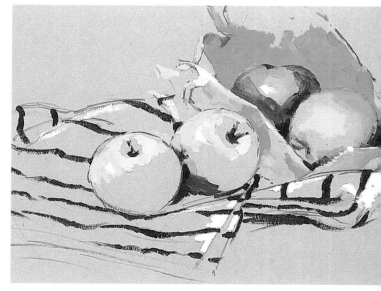

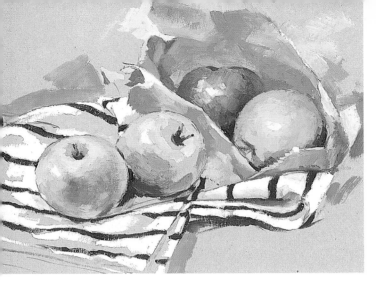

3 I noticed how the greens changed subtly from blue-greens to yellow-greens and translated that into the paint mixtures. I changed the colour on my brush constantly as I covered the surface of the apple. By now there were several different greens on my palette that I dipped in and out of. The same comparative process applied to the browns of the bag, made with Raw Umber, Burnt Sienna and touches of blue and white.

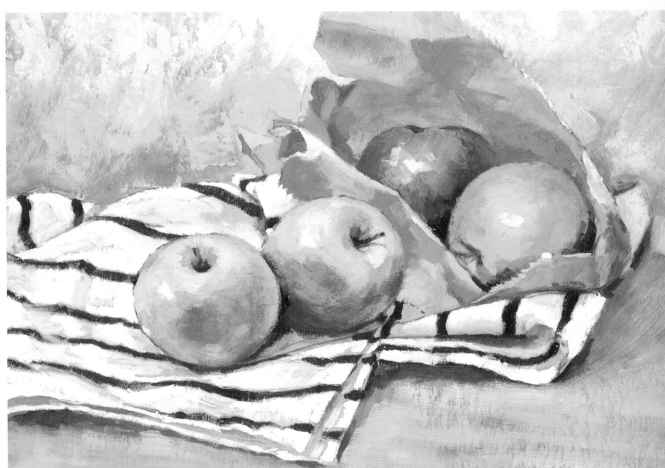

4 The shadows on the cloth were half supplied already by the buff board colour, so all I needed to do was to spread thin washes of very dilute white between the highlit areas to soften the shadows in between. I half closed my eyes to assess the background tone and brushed in a mixture of Prussian Blue, Titanium White and Raw Umber with bigger, flatter brushes and a palette knife. The colour on the table was dragged across the board roughly to retain the energy of the brushstrokes. Overpainting, and therefore muddiness, was avoided by careful colour mixing.

ABOVE: **Green Apples,** *25 x 36 cm (10 x 14 in), oil on board*

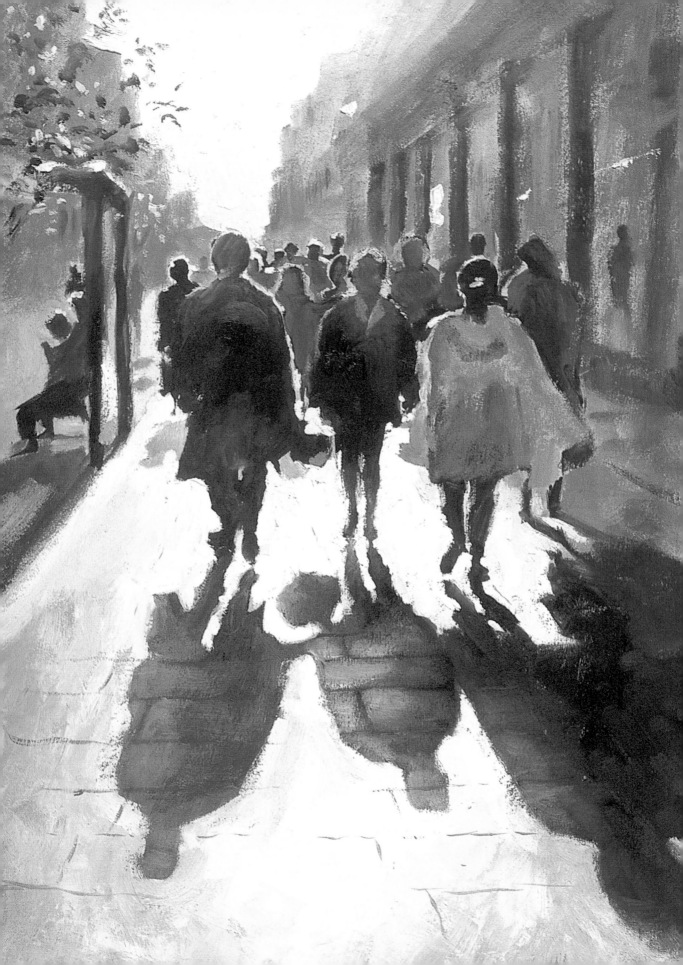

chapter 11

ABOUT TOWN

Outside the shelter of home a whole new wealth of subject matter awaits you. The urban environment seethes with painting ideas, limited only by your imagination and lack of accessibility beyond your control. If you have not painted outside before, or in areas populated by curious onlookers, you may need to pluck up courage to begin, but do not let fear of what others may think prevent you from enjoying such a bounty of subjects.

VISUAL SURPRISES

Townscapes are about man and his creations, on his scale. Sometimes they are magnificent, sometimes awful. But light can turn an ugly scene into a glorious panorama: write nothing off as an improbable subject. Be prepared to be surprised. Trust your own judgement; if something has kindled your interest it is a worthy subject for your brush.

Weather may greatly influence the choice of subject. On a sunny day the three-dimensional forms of buildings and the strong cast shadows will stand out. On grey days the view will be tonally flatter and inspiration will depend on receding tones and moving activities. Rain offers fascinating reflections, with the added bonus of repetition of the image above and below the ground line.

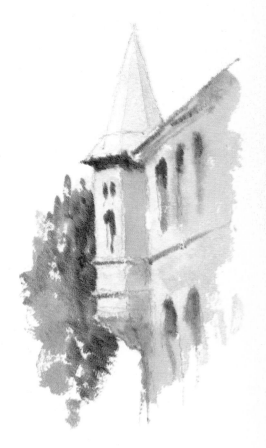

One must not imitate what one wants to create.

BRAQUE

OPPOSITE: **Rush Hour, Oxford Street,** *30 x 23 cm (12 x 9 in), oil on board*

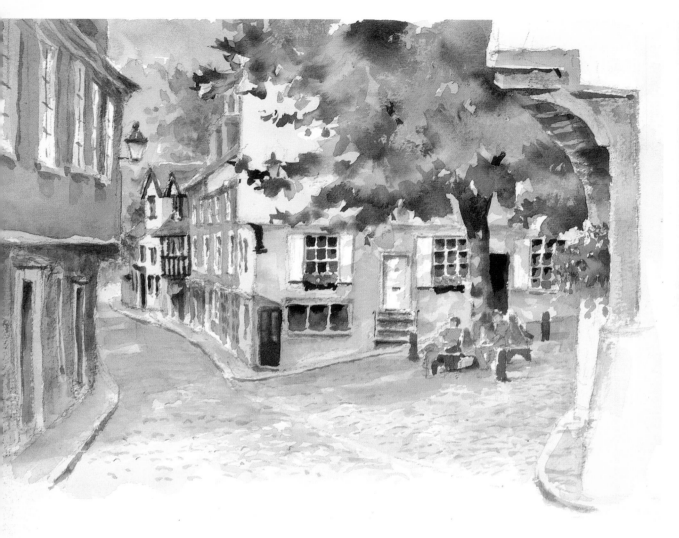

STREET LIFE SKETCHES

Start with a sketchbook; that way you will not feel so exposed, and you can perch on any railing or lean against any wall without having to find the perfect spot to lay out all your paints. A small palette, a size 5 sable brush and some water are all you need to make colourful sketches, or just use a pen, felt-tip, or pencil. Always make it easy on yourself rather than awkward.

Stop along the street, or sketch in cafés; sketch buildings, people shopping, chatting over coffee. Pull out your sketchbook on the bus or train or while waiting in a queue. Some will notice and be curious; if so just smile or look away casually and pretend you are painting someone or somewhere else. It feels like espionage and is all the more exciting because of it!

SETTING UP THE EASEL

Once you feel at home with sketching you can be more ambitious. Limit your materials to the essentials and if you are setting up an easel and stool think about the main passage of people before you

Elm Hill, Norwich

25 x 36 cm (10 x 14 in), watercolour
The perpendicular space between the two sides of the narrow road interested me. I liked the way the thin space opened into the courtyard and was narrowed again by the building on the right. I chose the limits of my composition through a viewfinder and started from a middle point — the left-hand white shutter.

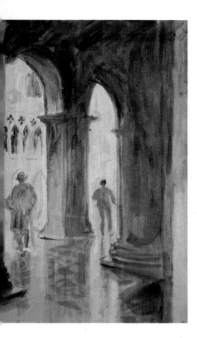

Passing the Time

28 x 20 cm (11 x 8 in), black and white acrylic on back of sketchbook
Even painting in the rain can be fun. Find some shelter and enjoy the reflections in the wet paving stones. Architecture does not have to be painted accurately to feel durable.

choose your site. Being 'in the way' will break your concentration and your view will often be blocked. I usually work with the sketchbook on my knee. Use your viewfinder to determine the composition, and step back from your sketch to check it works.

BUILDINGS

The linear characteristics of urban building offer some interesting design ideas for any painting. You can take a traditional perspective view along a street, or paint a façade head on, or look up at rooflines and chimneys.

A strong light source will make it easier to create solidity as you change the tone on the different angles of buildings, and lightening the tones of your buildings as they recede will create a sense of space and distance. You can alter the view to suit your composition. Lowering the height of buildings and reducing the number of windows is within the artist's power!

Shops with window displays and the darkness found under awnings create delicious dark tones at the base of buildings. To suggest reflections on glass vary the tone in the glass between the areas of reflected light on the surface and darker areas within. In oil and acrylic, and even in watercolour, you can lay a linear glaze of dilute white (or pale blue) over dried paint to suggest areas of reflected light.

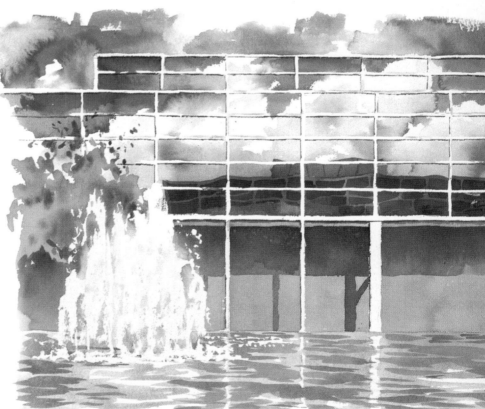

Queens Mall, Milton Keynes

41 x 51 cm (16 x 20 in), watercolour
The abstract patterns and geometric shapes of modern glass architecture are a fascinating subject, especially painting reflections in watercolour. Here the clouds are reinvented right across the front of the building.

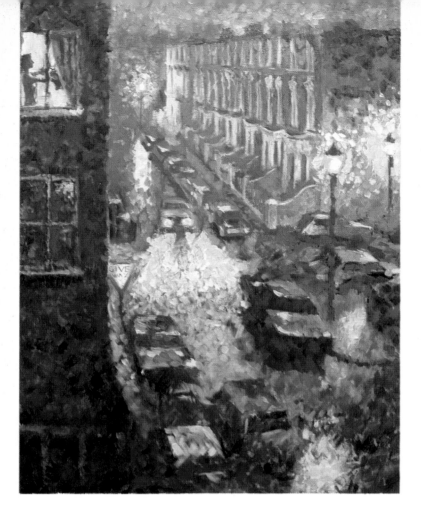

Parking Problems in Edith Terrace

122 x 76 cm (48 x 30 in),
oil on canvas
The view from my studio window in Chelsea had long attracted me, and finally one wet night I could wait no longer. Contrasting purple and yellow and using lively dabs of colour, I brought my mundane fascination to life.

VEHICLES

A bicycle always makes a good subject, leaning against a railing or propped by a wall, but cars, too, are fun to paint. There is always charm in the mundane; never ignore the images of your own urgent time. Impressionist paintings look nostalgic to us now, but they were thoroughly modern when painted.

Bright yellow and orange construction vehicles make great shapes and cranes look exquisite against the sky. Commercial vehicles, such as the yellow New York taxis and black London cabs or red buses, tell you the location of a painting without painting any of the tourist sites. Even road signs and lettering can be fun to paint, or can brighten up a dull painting.

PAINTING FIGURES

If you are including people in your painting vary the poses and colours. The overall shape of the figure counts, not what happens within it. There is usually no need to define feet and hands, nor faces, too clearly as this can tend to make the figure static; an indication or suggestion is enough.

Advancing or retreating figures can be indicated by simply showing one leg shorter than the other to suggest walking. If a figure is leaning unsupported the ankle carrying the weight will be in a line beneath the nape of the neck.

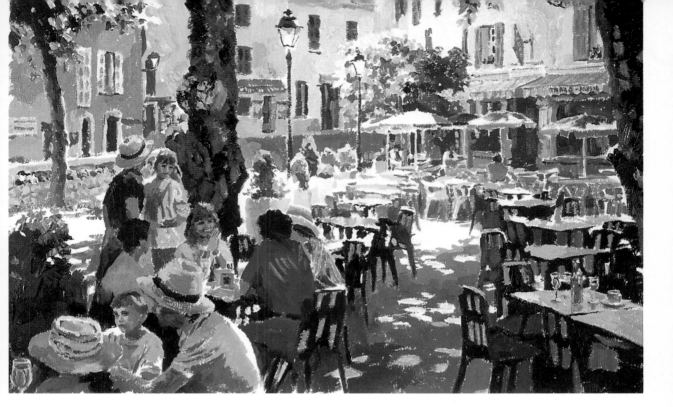

Café in Cavaillon

43 x 64 cm (17 x 25 in), oil on paper
*Planning your composition is even
more important if much is
happening in your picture. Here
the aisle between the tables leads the
eye through the dappled shade out
into the light beyond. Even though
the people are off to the left-hand
side they still remain the focus of
the painting.*

Crowds and groups of people in urban settings seem overwhelming at first, yet it is less difficult to portray figures en masse than to paint individuals: a few colourful blobs and lines will quickly render a throng of people. In any situation of intense activity pick out only that which interests you and either give it dominance in the foreground or just leave out the rest.

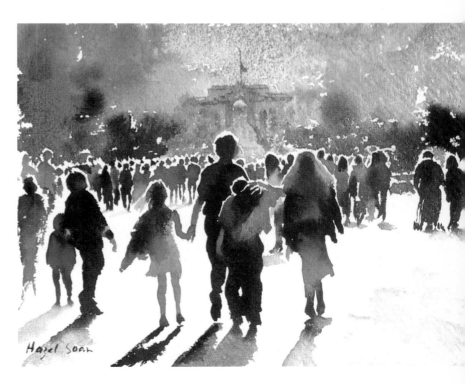

Multitude

13 x 18 cm (5 x 7 in), watercolour
*See how little detail is included in
this throng of people. The
numerous haloes of light and dark
blobs for bodies denote a crowd
that is barely painted and yet you
know is there.*

THE MOOD ON THE STREETS

Depending on the weather, the locale and the time of day, urban atmospheres can change tremendously. A building site or industrial sprawl may look dull in daytime, but is transformed at sunset: scaffolds, cranes and pylons turn into graceful silhouettes. The steam from cooling towers and the smoke from chimneys may not help the environment at large, but they create marvellous atmospherics for the painter.

Use the properties of colour and tone to evoke and enhance the mood you want to convey: light, bright colours for an upbeat ambience, cool, dark colours for a serious note.

School's Out

25 x 30 cm (10 x 12 in), acrylic on board
The temperature of colour can create atmosphere. In this painting the blues and whites evoke the chill of winter and the reds invite the cosy warmth of the children dressed against the cold.

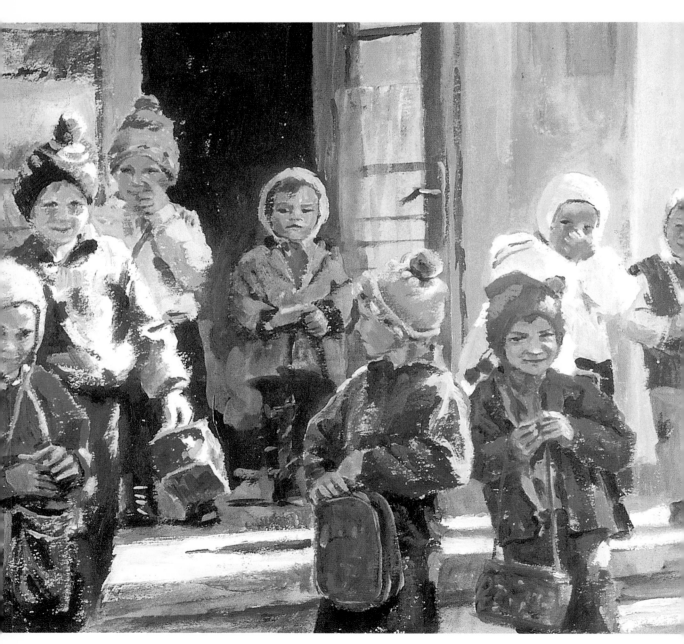

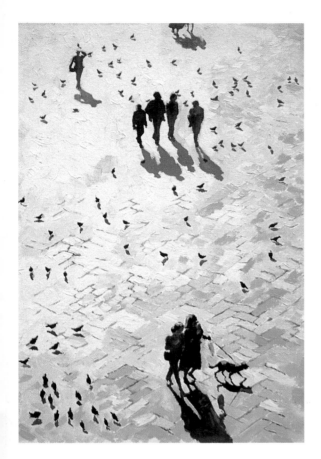

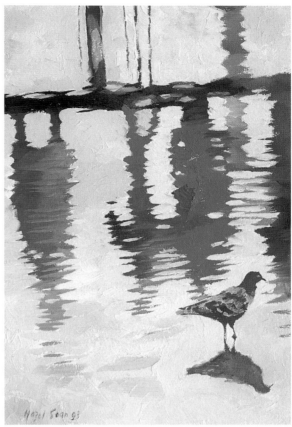

ABOVE: **Piazza San Marco**

28 x 20 cm (11 x 8 in), oil on canvas
Painting from a high viewpoint
creates interesting 'flat'
compositions on the picture plane.
This view looks down from the
campanile to the people and
pigeons crossing the piazza. The
long shadows take your eye across
the painting.

ABOVE RIGHT: **Pigeon in St
Mark's Square, acqua alto**

28 x 20 cm (11 x 8 in), oil on canvas
Here is another viewpoint. This
time it is at ground level, looking
down at the reflections of the people
crossing the catwalks laid out in
the piazza when the water is high.
Without the pigeon the composition
remains obscure.

ALTERNATIVE VIEWPOINT

Looking at things from different angles can be the catalyst for a painting. Looking down onto a view removes the necessity for a horizon level. The flattening of the perspective on the picture plane suggests a more abstract quality to the composition. Do not forget to look up too! You will see the patterns of urban skylines, the corners of buildings, chimney pots and tree tops, all starkly edged against the colour of the sky.

A WEALTH OF GREYS

On damp overcast days the urban landscape can look devoid of colour, almost grey. For the painter this is another opportunity. Mixing the three primary colours together (or two complementary colours), creates greys, browns and blacks. In oils and acrylics these can be lightened with white to create any tone, and in watercolour simply use water to dilute them.

The loveliest greys are made by mixing together colours that are not pure primaries, but between them hold some red, yellow and blue: try Burnt Sienna and French Ultramarine, or Alizarin Crimson and Viridian. Mixing two colours to make your grey enables you to veer the grey towards a particular colour more easily than if the grey comes straight from a tube. Remember you are licensed to exaggerate anything in the interests of the painting.

CHIMNEY POTS

COLOURS
Burnt Sienna
Cadmium Red
French Ultramarine
Raw Sienna
Titanium White

Urban skylines buzz with intriguing shapes, patterns, forms and colours. Homing in on some particular roofline feature makes an interesting painting subject. These chimney pots lit by the afternoon sun were several houses away. The strong tonal contrast combined with the distance made it easy for the eye to differentiate between the main shapes, but not get carried away with surface detail.

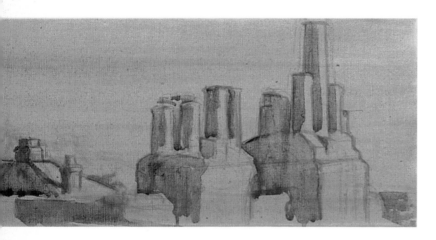

1 I stained the canvas with a wash of Burnt Sienna that matched the chimney-pot colour and gave a general underlying warmth to the painting. Being acrylic, this dried quickly. Onto this coloured ground I drew the outline shape of the roofline with a varying mixture of Cadmium Red and French Ultramarine, and washed in the areas of darkest tone.

2 Satisfied with the composition, I darkened the mixture of Cadmium Red and French Ultramarine and mapped in the dark areas more positively. I brushed in a line of Cadmium Red to blend together the dark and lighter sides of the rounded chimney pots. I indicated the brickwork with dilute washes and picked out the highlights with white mixed with a little Raw Sienna, exaggerating their brightness.

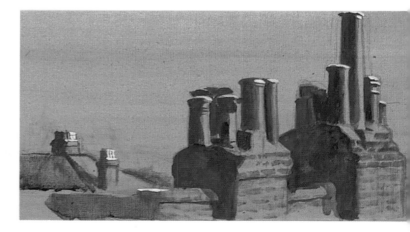

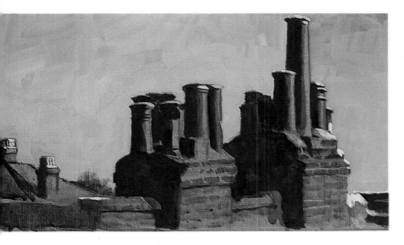

3 With a big flat brush and a mixture of French Ultramarine and Titanium White, I brushed in the shapes of the sky between and around the chimney stacks. Where pollution tinted the sky pink I did the same by adding a touch of Cadmium Red into the mixture. I laid a glaze of Raw Sienna over the brickwork to make it more yellow (another benefit of the fast-drying nature of acrylics).

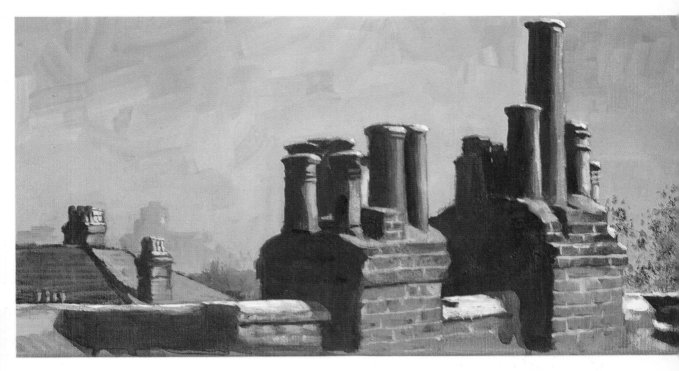

4 With a darker mixture of the red, blue and white, I suggested the hazy distant buildings and introduced the white copings along the roof ridge. At this point I felt that the painting could be finished, but then I decided to add more information. I painted the mortar lines between the brickwork and around the chimney-pot base with the Raw Sienna and white glaze. Standing back to look at the painting, I thought that the

right-hand corner looked empty of life, so I mixed Raw Sienna and French Ultramarine into a rich creamy mixture and, with a natural sponge, patted the colour onto the canvas to form foliage. I then decided the painting was finished.

ABOVE: **Chimney Pots,** *25 x 51 cm (10 x 20 in), acrylic on stained canvas*

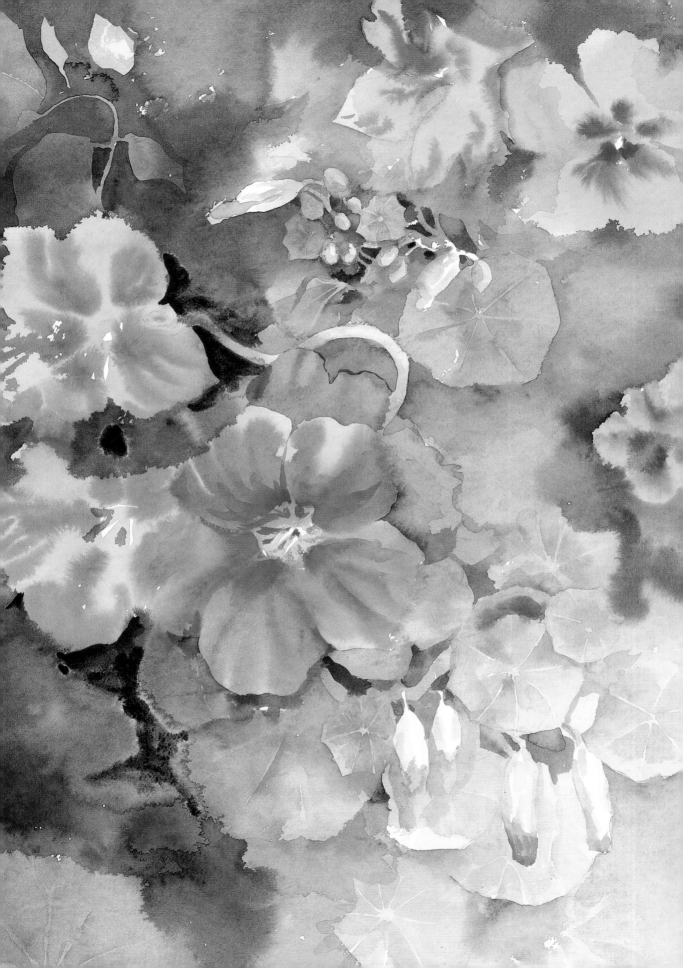

chapter 12

IN THE COUNTRY

Walking through the countryside we come across potential painting after painting. Divine creation offers endless subjects from vast panoramas to the thrill of a single leaf. Even where man adds his creation to that of nature the two seem to work in harmony as natural materials such as stone and wood rise upward in walls, fences and farm buildings. Ordered plantations are as charming as untamed woodland, while man-made canals are as fascinating as meandering rivers. And in addition to all these abundant riches we have the added bonus of changing seasons, where familiar landscapes are transformed into new and wonderful variations based on a similar theme.

ABUNDANT CHOICE

There is so much to choose from, and usually limited time. First, allow the eyes to roam and wander as you walk or drive through your landscape. Respond to the overall shape of a line of trees or buildings on the horizon. Look for an interesting bend in the road or the pattern of shadows across a track. Be aware of colours, such as the colour of the fields, one against the other, and the pattern they will make on the paper or canvas.

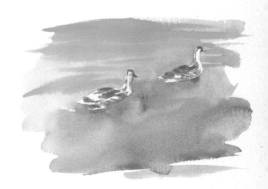

Nature contains the elements of all pictures ...
as the keyboard contains the notes of all music.
WHISTLER

Opposite: **Landscape Fragment,** *56 x 38 cm (22 x 15 in), watercolour*

DETAILS IN THE LANDSCAPE

Look down at your feet, up above your head, and into the undergrowth. The patterns on bark, a broken log, a few flowers caught in barbed wire or the doleful eyes of a tethered mule – these little details can be more significant than a classic landscape view.

The textures of weathered wood found on gate posts or old barn doors are a wonderful excuse to use textural effects such as wax resist, salt crystals and dry brush in watercolour, and combs and palette knife in oils and acrylics.

Explore the countryside for small details. You do not need to understand perspective, be able to paint skies or even make a composition: when your eyes alight upon the smallest area of interest indulge yourself in a painting of just that.

CHANGING LIGHT

The movement of the earth around the sun causes continual changes in the direction of the light source from the morning to the afternoon. If the sky is overcast the light tends to be more even, but as most of us prefer to go out painting on a warm sunny day this change in direction has to be addressed. You can, of course, paint several different paintings through the day to prevent you chasing the sun and its shadows.

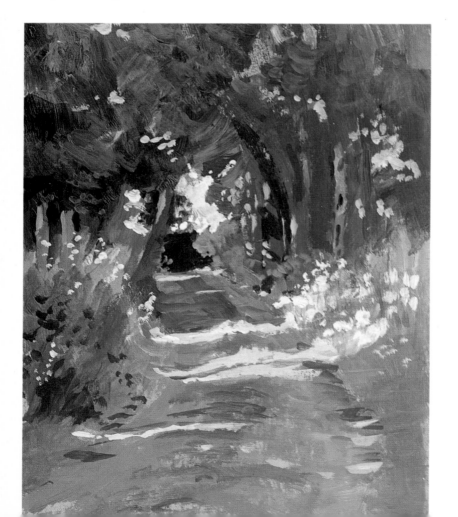

OPPOSITE: **Climbing Ivy**

15 x 10 cm (6 x 4 in), watercolour
In this small detail I found much enjoyment in picking out all the different greens of the foliage, easily seen under an overcast sky.

LEFT: **The Track**

25 x 18 cm (10 x 7 in), acrylic on board
Shadows and lights change really fast on sunny days. Before laying darks all over the painting I marked out the highlights across the path and on the grasses. These became obscured as the painting progressed, but were easy to retrieve over the fast-drying acrylic.

OPPOSITE: **The Great, Grey, Green, Greasy Limpopo**

23 x 30 cm (9 x 12 in), watercolour
Water in a landscape will usually reflect the colour of the sky, but the Limpopo in flood was mud coloured. The ochre-brown of the water and the blue of the sky mixed together made the perfect dull greens for the trees, preserving harmony in the painting.

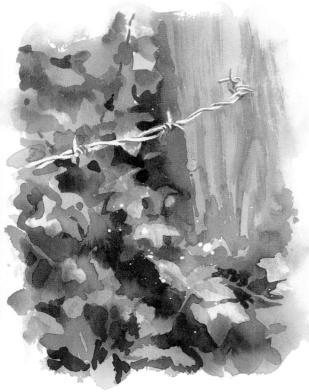

If you want to work on only one painting you need to apply visual memory, supplemented by sketches; otherwise you may invent an all-day light source that weakens the painting. Mapping in the shadows or areas of darker tone fairly near the start will help, especially in watercolour where tonal changes are hard to alter later in the painting. In oils and acrylics you can retouch whole areas and alter your tones completely, but with oils they will become muddy, so it is still wise to decide on the light direction you will paint at an early stage.

DULL DAYS

Dull days have their advantages for artists. Not only do they supply a more even light, but the subtle variations in colour, especially among greens, show up more clearly without strong light and shadows to obscure them. Hue rules when there is little tonal contrast. You will notice how reds stand out more on dull days than they do in sunshine.

Whereas a photograph might look dull on a low light day, an artist can see and bring to our attention both colour and tonal difference to make it appear more lively. Even subtle variations in colour and tone are attractive in the painted image.

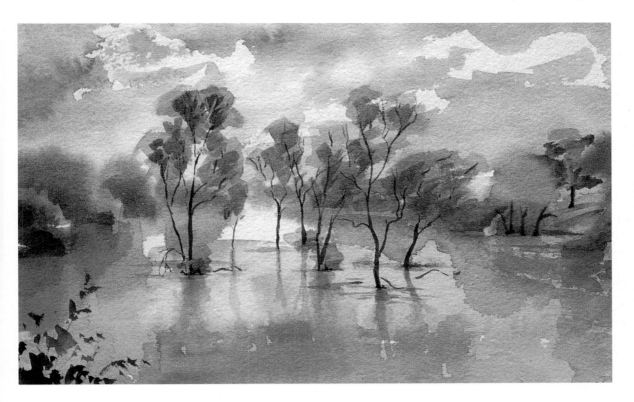

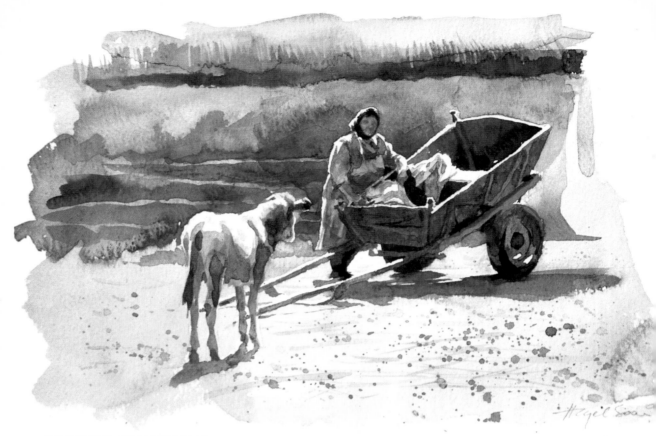

BRIGHT SUNSHINE

Before you choose your subject on a sunny day, look in both directions; sometimes the view looking into the sun is more exciting than the obvious sunlit view. The tonal difference between the areas cast in shadow and the dancing highlights can make a livelier painting.

Look at the colour of the shadows and how they link to the objects that cast them. Allow your shadows to run or trickle out from their objects, so that the two are united in colour and tone and not painted as two separate items.

GREENS

Many landscapes tend to a preponderance of green. In watercolours greens are best mixed from blues and yellows/ochres/siennas, so that even within the mixing slight variations occur. If there are many different greens to be painted it helps to link them with the same blue; that way harmony exists as the blue is common to all. In oils, however, I find the most vibrant greens are usually found ready mixed from the tubes. Other colours in the painting can then be added to these greens to make their darker tones.

Remember to view your foliage as forms rather than individual leaves. A flat brush in oils will help you paint your greenery in blocks rather than dabs, and wet-in-wet washes in watercolour will stop you fussing over details. Sponges can also be used to give light foliage a random look.

A Hard Life

20 x 28 cm (8 x 11 in), watercolour
The calf's legs and the cartwheel are painted so the colours are continued into their shadows, connecting the two.

Three Men in a Wagon

15 x 15 cm (6 x 6 in), white gouache and black watercolour on brown paper
Simplicity of expression, as in this tonal sketch, is often the best way to paint something that touches you.

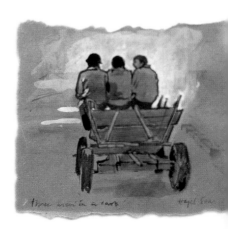

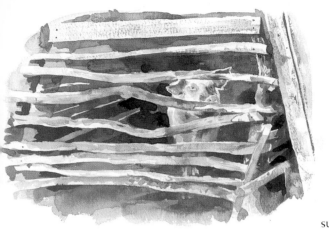

ATMOSPHERE

Landscapes have atmospheres, often bound together by a predominant colour, perhaps a cool blueness, or a warm ochre tint. For overall warmth, paint with warm colours, reds and oranges, and yellows and blues that veer towards red. You can tint your canvas, board or paper with a colour appropriate to the painting. In watercolour this could be a dilute wash over the paper on which you paint subsequent washes, perhaps a warm Yellow Ochre. In acrylics an underwash of Burnt Sienna will lend warmth to a picture.

For a cool atmosphere use cool blues and blue-greens, cold yellows, mauves, umbers and greys. The undercolour can again be quite strong, but pale blues and greys can be helpful if there is a large area of light sky.

Since oils and acrylics are opaque it is exciting to build highlights and darks onto a mid tone appropriate to the mood of your painting. You can even use rich dark colours under your painting or use the natural colour of linen canvas. As oil tints take a while to dry you can use a thin acrylic wash as an undercolour and still paint with oils on top.

Piggy in the Middle

20 x 28 cm (8 x 11 in), watercolour
Mood in painting is helped by using a limited palette. Here Yellow Ochre, French Ultramarine and Alizarin Crimson create a warm atmosphere.

Look Right, Look Left

20 x 28 cm (8 x 11 in), watercolour
Prussian Blue, a cooler blue than French Ultramarine, is mixed with the same red and yellow as above and creates a very different mood.

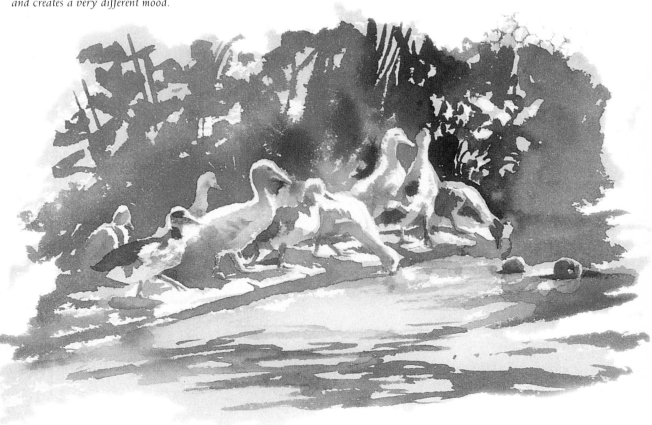

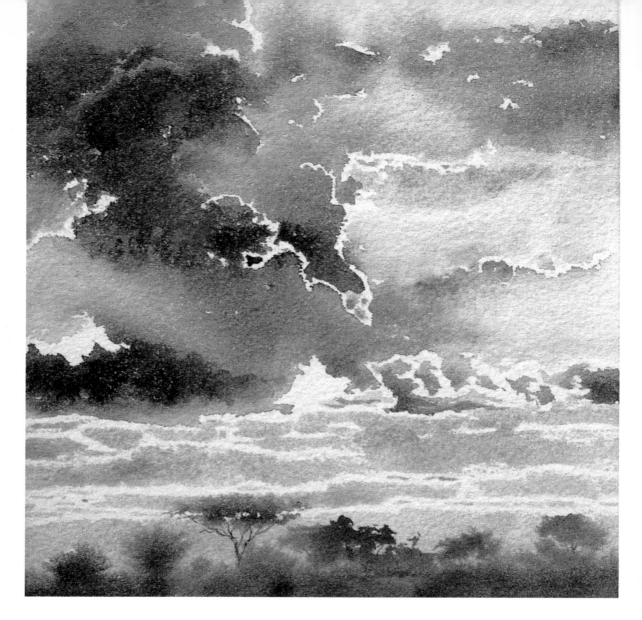

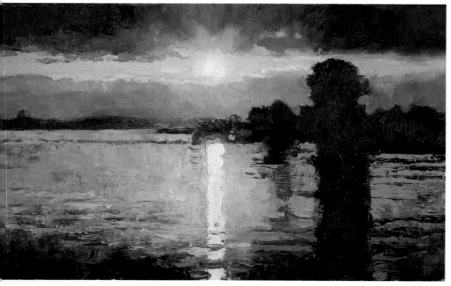

ABOVE: **Cumulonimbus**
*16.5 x 15.5 cm (6½ x 6 in),
watercolour*
Wet-in-wet blends of watercolour
are perfect for cloud formations.
Dark tones for the shadowy bases
can be touched into wet washes
and allowed to spread.

LEFT: **Liquid Gold**
20 x 33 cm (8 x 13 in), oil on board
The reflection of the sky in water
makes a strong composition as the
similarity of the top and bottom
halves of the painting create an
almost abstract quality on the
picture plane.

SKIES

The sky above the landscape is an integral part of the scene. Never be afraid of placing colour in the sky, even if it appears almost white. Bring whatever colours you use in the sky into the landscape below to keep sky and land united.

The sky nearer the land is often lighter than the sky above your head. This variation in tone, from lighter up to darker, will give a sense of space and distance to the aerial canopy arching over the landscape. You will also find that a blue sky is often darker in tone than you think, so check it against the lightest areas of the composition, especially those that are against the sky such as chimney pots and highlit foliage.

EVENTS

In general people or animals add life and focus to a painting, and events taking place in the country add interest to a generally passive subject.

Sporting occasions, local fiestas, riding events or fêtes are a rich resource of action if you have the courage to attempt them. Try not to be too ambitious; just enjoy the atmosphere and fill the pages of your sketchbook. If you are brave enough to try a full painting, take time over your composition and drawing to familiarize yourself with the subject before venturing into colour.

Cricket Match in the Stour Valley

18 x 25 cm (7 x 10 in), watercolour
In this half-hour sketch painted at a cricket match the figures are marked with a pencil and left out of the hedge wash as vague white paper shapes. Watercolour is great for speed.

EN PLEIN AIR

Painting outside in the open air is special whatever the results you achieve. You become lost in concentration, and yet completely aware of every nuance of changing light and knowing the passage of the clouds without looking up. Time passes unaccounted: asked how long your painting took, the chances are you do not know. When you return home the satisfaction felt is beyond measure.

OVER TO YOU...

Instead of painting one view in the landscape go into the countryside and find a pleasant location. Look at the small fragments that belong to it, move close to them and spend an hour or two painting as many details as you have time for. I prefer working in watercolour outside, but use whatever medium you find most convenient.

> **Motto**
> Be unpredictable.

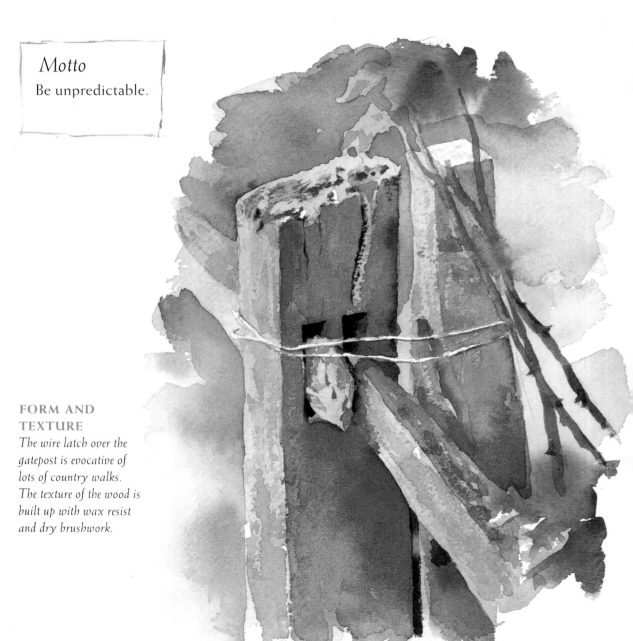

FORM AND TEXTURE
The wire latch over the gatepost is evocative of lots of country walks. The texture of the wood is built up with wax resist and dry brushwork.

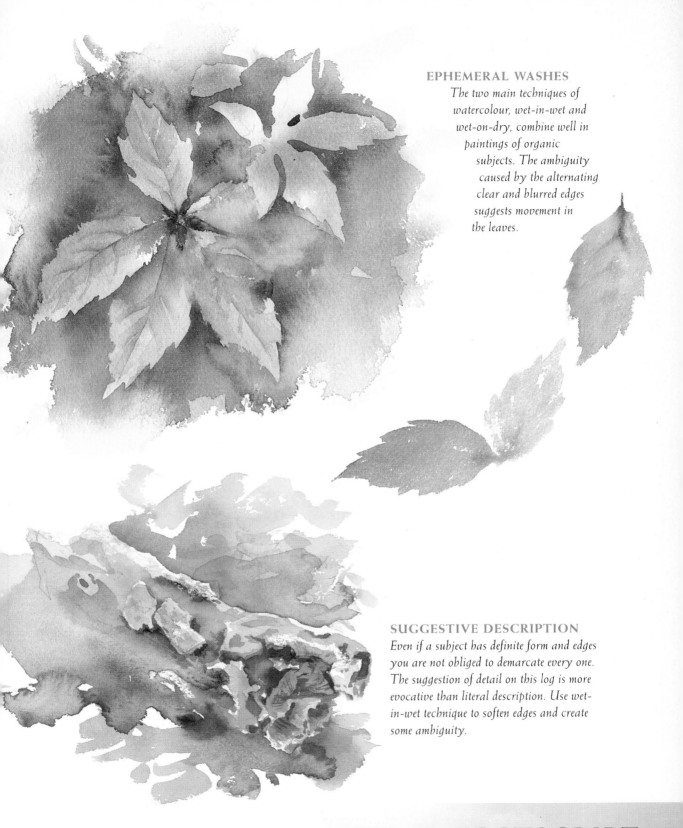

EPHEMERAL WASHES

The two main techniques of watercolour, wet-in-wet and wet-on-dry, combine well in paintings of organic subjects. The ambiguity caused by the alternating clear and blurred edges suggests movement in the leaves.

SUGGESTIVE DESCRIPTION

Even if a subject has definite form and edges you are not obliged to demarcate every one. The suggestion of detail on this log is more evocative than literal description. Use wet-in-wet technique to soften edges and create some ambiguity.

POSTSCRIPT

Lay all your paintings in a group. Do they sggest the character of the landscape better, as well as, or less well than if you had painted the whole scene?

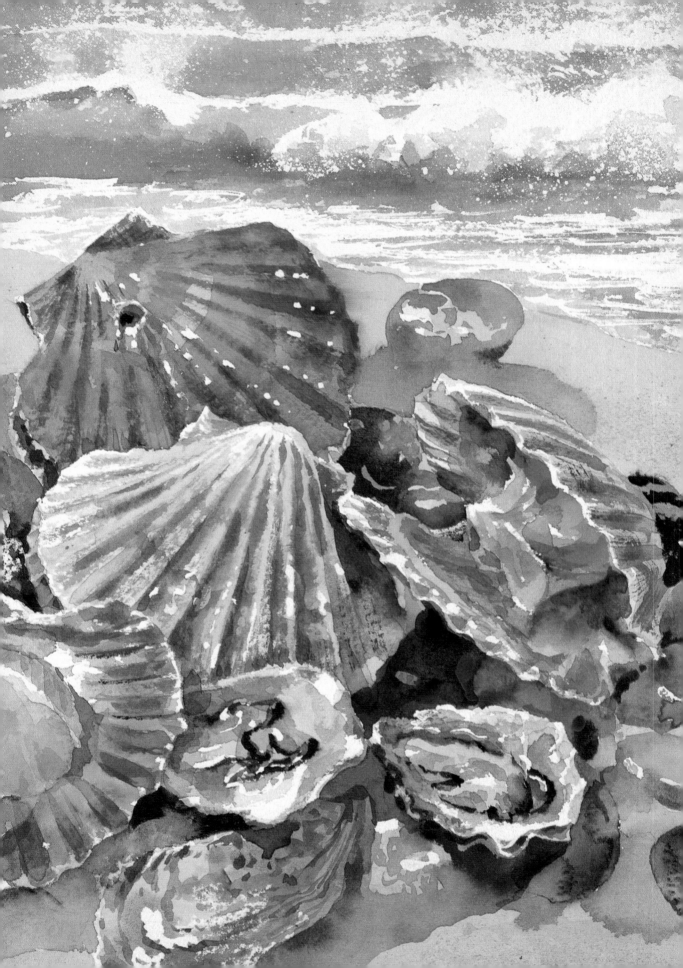

chapter 13

BY THE SEA

The uncluttered views across the sea and seashore are a dream for the artist who likes simplicity. Like the desert, the vast open expanses are dotted with occasional isolated features and events, creating drama amidst calm, presence in emptiness.

The threefold division of sky, sea and beach makes a satisfactory compositional format and the wonderful treasure chest of driftwood, pebbles, rocks and dunes provides endless interest for the brush.

BE PREPARED

The simplicity inherent in open seascapes encourages the artist to keep it simple, both in painting and in equipment. The pleasure of being by the sea, hearing the waves, with toes in the sand or curled over a rock, adds to the delight of taking brushes and paints to the seaside. The only enemy can be the wind, which hurls sand at the best of oils and lifts the paper from under the watercolour. Come prepared with bulldog clips, large rubber bands and patience, and even a stiff breeze will not deter you!

A rug or towel to sit on will help prevent sand blowing into the paint on your palette. However, if that happens, just use it as real texture in your painting.

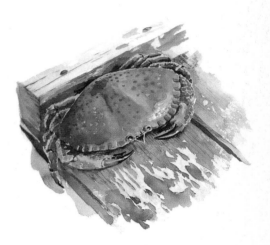

The environment is the composition.

KANDINSKY

OPPOSITE: **Oysters and Scallops,** *26.5 x 19 cm (10½ x 7½ in), watercolour*

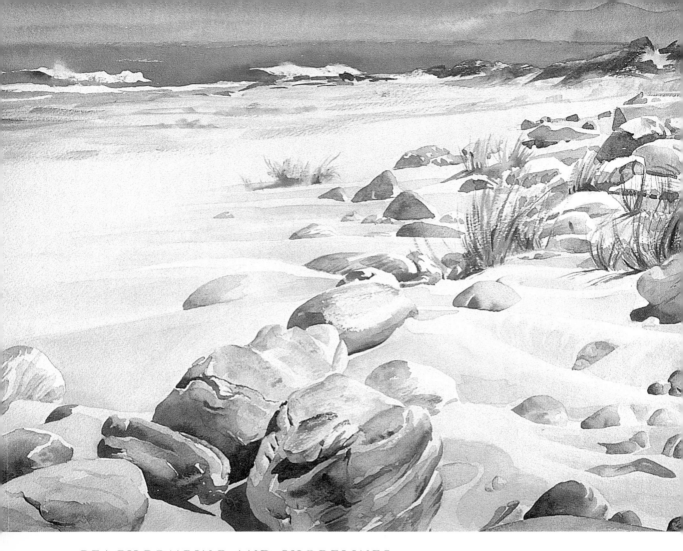

BEACHCOMBING AND SHORELINES

Along every shoreline lies a plethora of abandoned shells, sea life and debris from the deep. The colours and textures of these items are delightful to paint. Shells present boundless colours and shapes that are especially good for the watercolourist. Driftwood from fishing boats also tells a story.

Each beach is characterized by unique features, battered groynes, rock pools or abandoned spades. You need only paint these items as still lifes on their own and let memory and imagination dream of the settings.

For a seascape position your viewpoint to bring chosen features into focus, making them large in the foreground. Dune grasses, for example, bending in the wind, tell you about the openness of the beach, the strong breezes, the sandy dunes; lower your eye level to allow them to dominate the foreground.

ROCKS AND STONES

If you look closely you will see that all the colours and patterns under the sun reside in a handful of pebbles washed up on the shore. Rotund boulders, much larger in size, come in hundreds of different shapes with seams of quartz and granite to pattern their

Next Stop, Brazil

41 x 51 cm (16 x 20 in), watercolour
The illusion of great distance can be suggested by the ever-reducing size of stones as they recede into the background. The narrowing of the beach on the picture plane also aids the impression of distance.

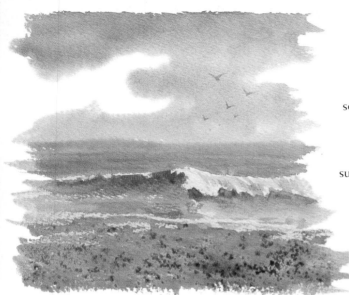

surfaces. Then come huge rocks, round and friendly, sharp and angry, their deep fissures demanding strong indigos and sepias neat from the tube.

The three-dimensionality of rocks and stones make them excellent material for practising the gradations of tone across a surface to make something look round. Once form is in place concentrate on surface details, texture or pattern.

THE SEA ITSELF

Paintings of the sea itself can be really interesting, especially if there is implied movement. In watercolour leave the white paper for the foam, or scratch the surface of the paper to reveal white from underneath a wash. In oils and acrylics you have marvellous opaque white paint that can be ladled on with a palette knife or brushed on with swift, energized strokes to create the spume and spray of the churning sea.

Waves themselves make a fascinating subject. Watch the rise and fall, the ebb and flow for a while before deciding the shape of the waves you want to paint. You cannot paint them all; you must choose, and then summarize. Look closely at the colour of the rising wave – the translucent viridians, the green-golds of the water before it curls over and crashes down in milky whites.

The Wave

20 x 23 cm (8 x 9 in),
The head-on wave crashes onto a beach that has real texture, produced by using sugar.

The Wild Sea

56 x 76 cm (22 x 30 in), oil on paper
Strong tonal compositions can be painted along shorelines where limited local colour readily takes on shades of greys.

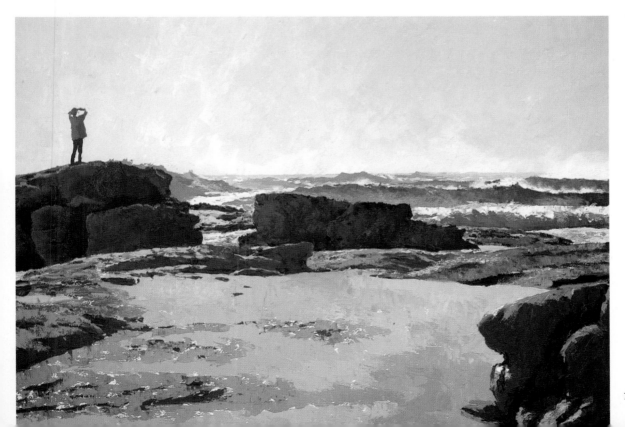

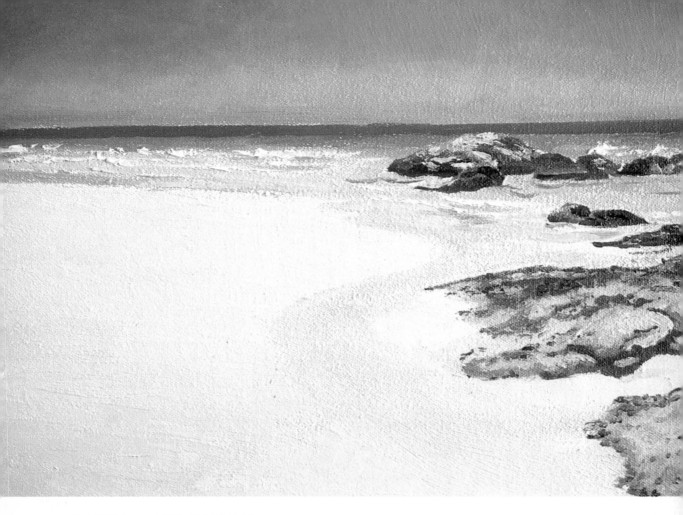

PANORAMIC VISION

The 360-degree vision that beach scenes offer the artist often makes it hard to decide on the subject to paint. Wide, empty spaces and stretches have commanding atmospheres, and can be kept really simple. Alternatively, look for a focal point of interest, such as a line of groynes, a large rock, figures, a dog running, or a shapely wave.

Use your viewfinder and quick line sketches of potential layouts to assure yourself the composition is not boring, too predictable or complacent. If in doubt try raising or lowering the horizon line. More sky might have more impact than more beach.

ATMOSPHERICS

With brooding skies and stormy waters, inclement weather makes a great subject for the sea painter. Use limited colours and ensure that the sky colour is reflected in the sea to keep the areas above and below the horizon in harmony.

If you want to create a sense of distance use the fact that cool colours recede and warm colours advance. 'Blueing' colours in the background can enhance the sense of space. The intervention of the atmosphere changes and pales colours, so remember to lighten the tones and soften the hues from the foreground to the background, even in the overhead sky.

Ocean Stream

20 x 28 cm (8 x 11 in), oil on canvas
The same sense of exhilarating calm felt by being near the sea in real life can be created in an uncluttered painting. That a small flat board daubed with a few colours can give a sense of wide, open space is, to me, still amazing.

River of Gold

91 x 91 cm (36 x 36 in), oil on canvas
Indian Yellow is a really hot
yellow, ideal for the colour of the
setting sun. The small boy bending
to the stream of the tide gives scale
to this atmospheric painting.

Just as a figure can bring life to a landscape, so ships and boats make excellent focal points for paintings of the sea. Quick sketches of sailing yachts, tankers and ships as they go by can be gathered on a separate piece of paper so that you can choose their position in your composition without feeling rushed. The cheerful colours of fishing boats and container ships make delightful subjects, and all the paraphernalia that surrounds commercial or fishing ports make them lucrative hunting ground for the artist.

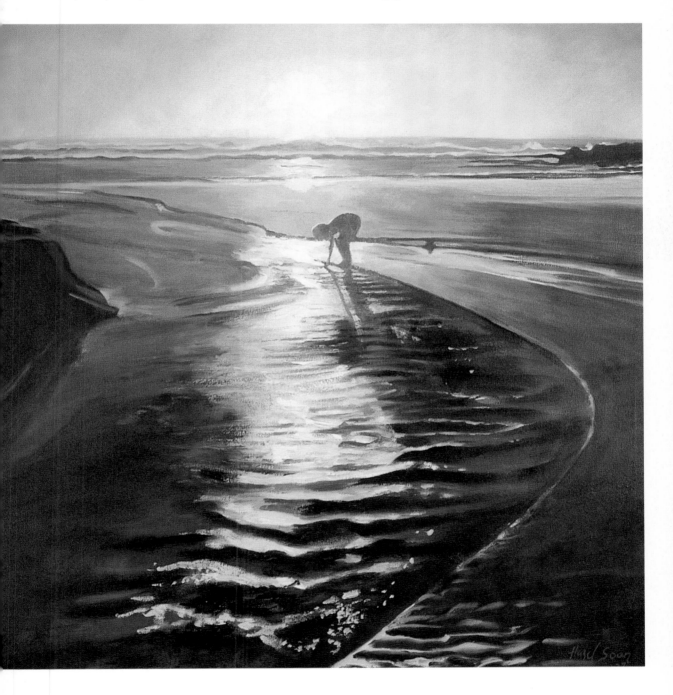

FISHING BOATS

COLOURS
Prussian Blue
Cadmium Red
Cadmium Yellow
Viridian
Coeruleum
Cobalt Blue
Yellow Ochre

Fishing boats are fun to paint because of their interesting shapes and vibrant colours. I homed in on just three bobbing gently by the jetty. The definition inside the hull and the blur of reflections around the hull allow the watercolourist the chance to use a happy combination of wet-in-wet washes and wet-on-dry brushwork.

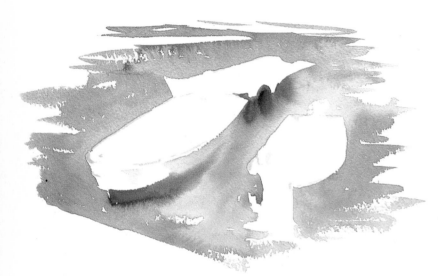

1 The boats are quite specific shapes, so I made a careful pencil outline of the hulls relative to each other and used a little masking fluid on the gunwales. I washed in Prussian Blue for the surrounding sea and shaded sides of the hulls, plunging Cadmium Red into the wet paint beneath the forward hull and allowing it to spread softly as a reflection.

2 I mixed Cadmium Red and Prussian Blue together to make the rich darks of the insides of the hulls. I reserved the shapes of the seat planks from the washes. The yellow boat was full of boating clutter, so I indicated this with wet-in-wet washes and reserved highlights.

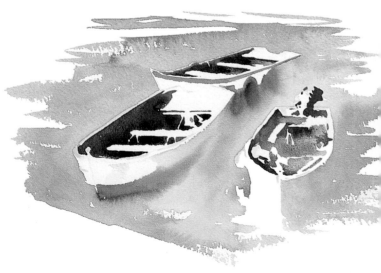

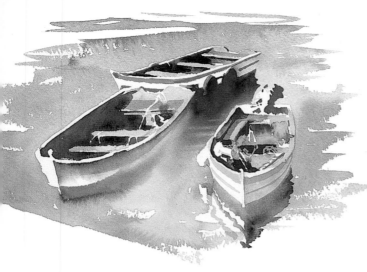

3 Once the forms were established I could start on the surface features. I painted the stripes on the yellow boat with Cadmium Yellow and Yellow Ochre. I painted the reflection at the same time by brushing the dark water colour up against the wet ochre of the bottom stripe and allowed the colours to merge. I touched in the colours of the seat planks with Viridian and Cobalt Blue.

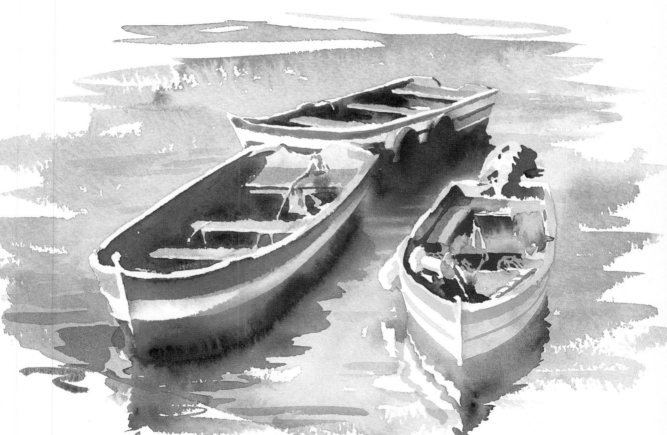

4 The deep, dark reflection under the furthermost boat links the three boats together. I brushed this in with Prussian Blue, wetting the area between the boats so that it would blend into the blue already there. As it dried I lifted out the ripples horizontally with the tip of the brush. I painted the stripes on the other two boats, carefully following their form. Finally, I brushed a few ripples across the blue wash to ruffle the sea.

ABOVE: **Fishing Boats,** 28 x 36 cm (11 x 14 in), watercolour

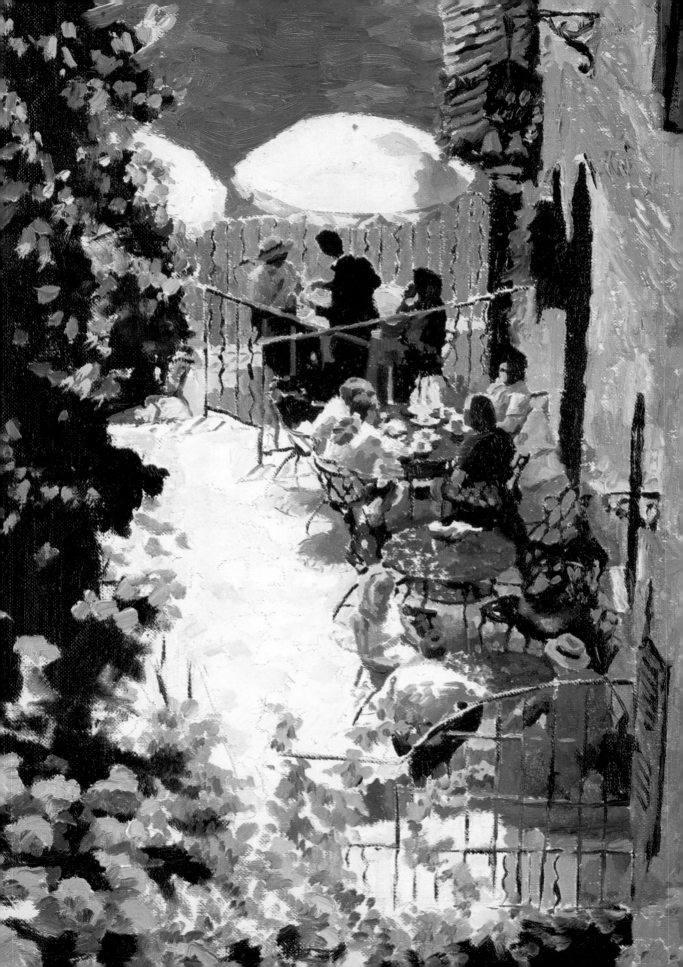

chapter 14

ON HOLIDAY

For some people the only real time they have available to paint is on holiday. Happily this is usually a time of new inspirations and fair weather and it therefore offers boundless subject matter for the painter.

There are always the obvious painting choices, such as famous buildings and striking landscapes. Certainly, remarkable architecture and memorable places are good subjects and are frequently painted as a result, but trying to paint them in a slightly different way from the usual view can be a more exciting challenge.

There are also less predictable images that may evoke your holiday in a more personal way, as well as countless other subjects that are part of holiday experiences and which can make fun paintings and wonderful memories.

TRAVELLING LIGHT

First, you have to decide which medium to use and which materials to carry. Some airlines will no longer allow the carriage of oil paint, but in any case I favour the use of watercolour on holiday because it is light to carry, dries quickly and is clean to use in hotel rooms or someone else's home. The pigment mixes with easily available water and watercolour paper packs flat.

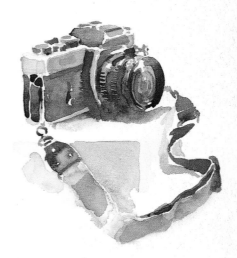

The time to relax is when you don't have time to relax.

ANON

OPPOSITE: **Eze,** *51 x 41 cm (20 x 16 in), oil on canvas*

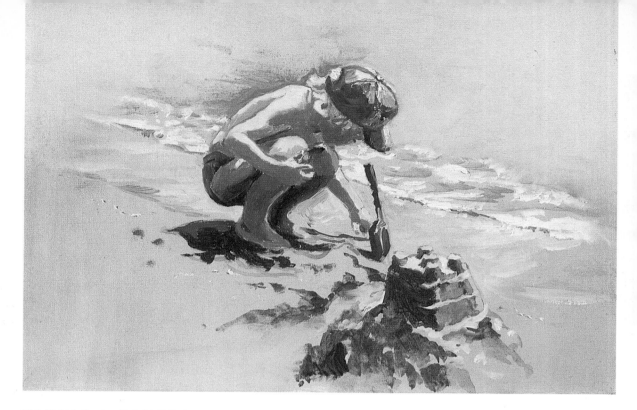

TAKING A CAMERA

The camera can be an invaluable tool on holiday. Film is cheap compared to time, so ensure you have plenty of reference photographs to work from on your return. If you have a long lens, zoom in on details from a distance and look through the lens as you would a viewfinder.

When you paint from the photographs beware of being a slave to the image. As with real life look for a balance of tones and an interesting composition within the photograph itself.

FAMILY FUN

Children playing in the sand and sea are an all-time favourite subject. They are even more charming if they are your own, so take the sketchbook to the beach and make a few small paintings. Figures in stretching, crouching or bending poses, dressed in swimming costumes are as good as going to life classes!

Look for the shape of the pose, reflections in wet sand, and the immediate setting. Or just paint the buckets and spades – their bright plastic primary colours will add zest to any sketchbook.

SUNSHINE AND SHADOWS

The patterns of strong contrasts created between light and shade make interesting subjects. Blazing sunshine and whitewashed walls give plenty of opportunities to the watercolourist for using the brightness of the white paper as the lightest highlights.

Always look at the colour of shadows. On white walls they are usually blue or mauve and seldom grey. On terracotta tiles the shadows are hot reddish browns. In oils and acrylics a glaze of colour over a dull shadow will soon enrich it.

ABOVE: **Castles in the Sand**
20 x 25 cm (8 x 10 in),
oil on tinted canvas
Children grow so fast, and change so quickly, but sketches such as this, which are quick to do on the spot or from holiday photos, can catch a moment forever. Do not be too ambitious; leave out everything but the essentials, and you have a poignant little painting.

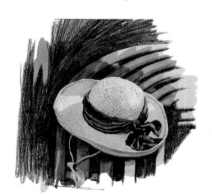

Hat on Deck
15 x 15 cm (6 x 6 in),
watercolour and conté crayon
Light colours that are often bleached out by bright sun look richly coloured in shade.

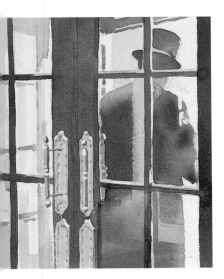

The Doorman

18 x 18 cm (7 x 7 in), watercolour
Hotels, restaurants and bars never seem to mind the presence of an artist. This image through the door of the Ritz Club is evocative; a sense of mystery is created by small areas of obscurity behind reflected glass.

WINDOWS, HOTELS AND ROOMS

Windows have a great sense of personality and place. Painting just the window of a building makes an interesting subject, and one that can be completed in a short time on holiday.

Henri Matisse and Pierre Bonnard often painted the view through the window, incorporating the balcony, window frame or part of the room into the painting. This view within a view makes an interesting double composition and holiday apartments and hotels may offer the perfect opportunity to try this out. Assess the tone of the room against the view to check their relative values and create a sense of 'throughness' from one world to another.

What about the hotel itself? When it rains, do you retire to the bar and drown your sorrows in sangria or, instead, open the paintbox and paint the lobby or the hotel room. David Hockney made numerous coloured crayon and pen and ink sketches in various Californian hotel rooms. Some included his friends, some his clothes draped on chairs, some just a corner of the room. Along with his pictures of swimming pools and boulevards these paintings not only please the eye and aesthetic senses, but they also evoke an era, a time and a place.

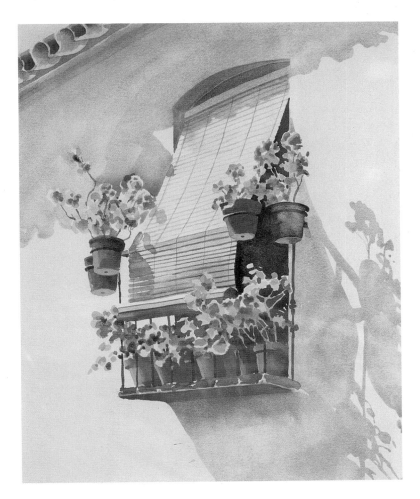

Window in Estepona

46 x 36 cm (18 x 14 in), watercolour
In the Mediterranean region highly decorated windows become real-life paintings and sculptures. The strong blue shadows add a touch of drama to a pretty subject.

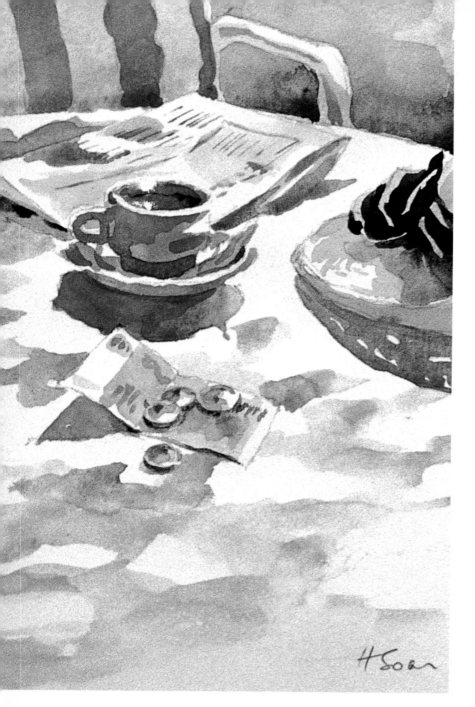

Seizing the Moment
18 x 13 cm (7 x 5 in), watercolour
On holiday companions sit for a long time over beers and coffee, watching the world go by. Now you have time to paint the people, the café, the empty coffee cups, or even the bill and change on the saucer, while sitting comfortably at the table enjoying good company.

OPPOSITE: **Roofs in Villefranche**
20 x 28 cm (8 x 11 in), oil on paper
The generous palms and red tile roofs so typical of the South of France epitomize for me the cheerful atmosphere of the Mediterranean towns. There were several vantage points to look down on Villefranche, but, for me, the church tower made the perfect focal point for a painting.

CARPE DIEM

You may find yourself with friends who are not interested in waiting for you to finish a painting. If this is the case seize the moments when you are all at rest; for example, sunbathing on the beach, sipping beers or coffee, or taking a siesta. Tans fade, memories do not, and you will not regret the time spent painting.

HOLIDAY CHARACTERISTICS

Different places have different characteristics that in some way evoke or sum up the location. When you are choosing views to paint look for whatever it is that in your opinion most aptly

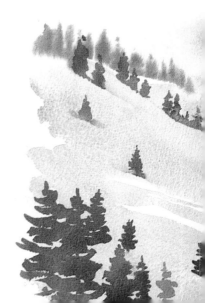

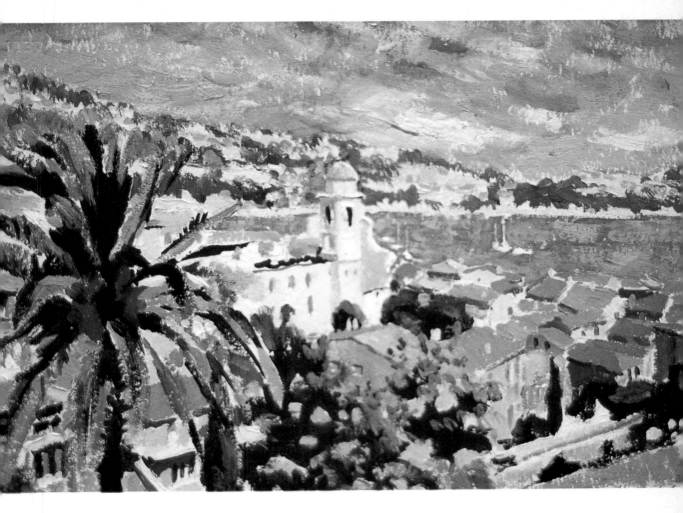

BELOW: **The Slopes**

20 x 28 cm (8 x 11 in), watercolour
If you have little time to paint here is an ideal subject. Simply mix up dull greens for the trees and blues for the shadows and say it all in a few brushstrokes!

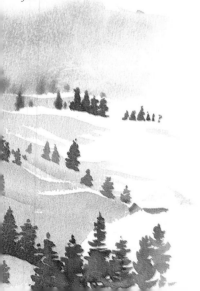

portrays the essence of the place. It could be the predominant colour or patterns of the brickwork, the type of vehicles, the species of trees or local crafts and customs. Trying to paint the spirit of the locale makes you look more thoughtfully at the visual inspiration and adds weight to your paintings.

WINTER HOLIDAYS

Here is a great subject for watercolourists: reserving the white paper for snowy landscapes!

If watercolour freezes it makes the most lovely patterns on the paper as it thaws, and numb fingers are a small price to pay for such texture.

Acrylics offer the enjoyment of working from dark to light and in oils few colours are needed, which enables the artist to keep the painting crisp and clean. Tone is of utmost importance as the virgin whites dazzle the eyes. Lay your brush strokes with thought to the lie of the land, so that they help describe the contours of the white landscape. The elongated turquoise and blue shadows cast by the low winter sun add to the already strong compositional possibilities of dramatic tonal contrast.

OVER TO YOU...

This is your holiday, so whatever you do must be fun and relaxing. Take a sketchbook and fill it with different visual notes, incidents and anything to do with your holiday. Do not worry about composition or finish; just use your paintbrush as your eyes.

Motto
You get back
what you put in.

THE PERSONAL TOUCH
watercolour
Look around for items that have been part of your holiday in a less obvious way; it could be sunglasses and a coke can, a hat and flip-flops, the hotel bill or an 'in' joke re some irritation. Make some small paintings of these memories.

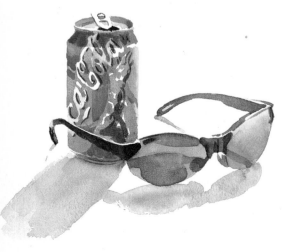

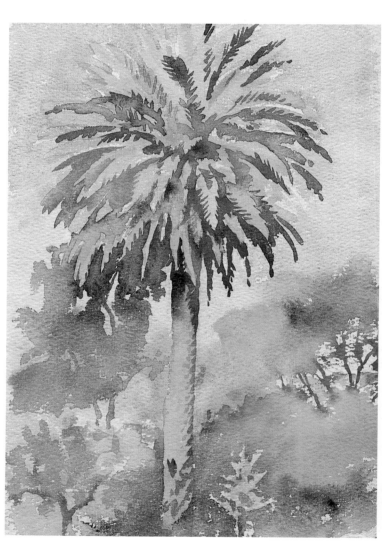

ENHANCING OBSERVATION
25 x 20 cm (10 x 8 in), watercolour
This splendid palm tree overlooked the swimming pool at a hotel I was staying in. Some palms are quite elegant, some scruffy and some amusing. There is usually a variety of greens to mix, so try different yellows with different blues and greens straight from the tube.

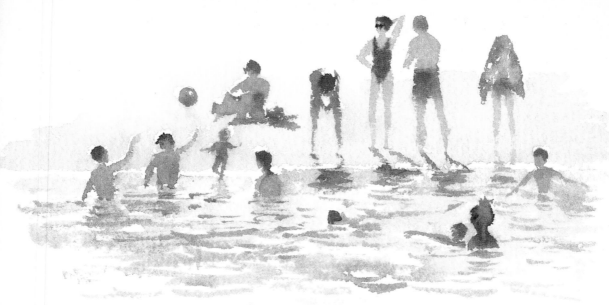

CATCHING THE ACTION

watercolour

People on beaches make great life models. As one moves off another takes up a similar pose. Sketch as many different poses as you can as quickly as you can. Look at overall shape and do not worry about detail.

LOADED BRUSHSTROKES

watercolour

Painting the shape of something with one colour only is also satisfying. The tip of the brush started at the beak and then the body of the brush was pressed down to release paint for the torso and lifted up again to the tip for the feet – so just one brush stroke.

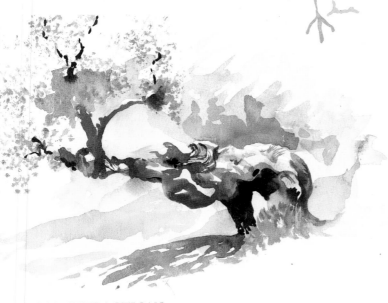

LOCAL ATTRACTIONS

watercolour

A quick stop by the roadside affords only enough time to look at the shape of this twisted olive tree, but even painting this half-finished study was enjoyable and I had the chance to really look at the bark of the tree.

POSTSCRIPT

Have you enjoyed painting the subjects you chose? Was anything too laborious? Were you under any obligation to put in something you would rather have left out?

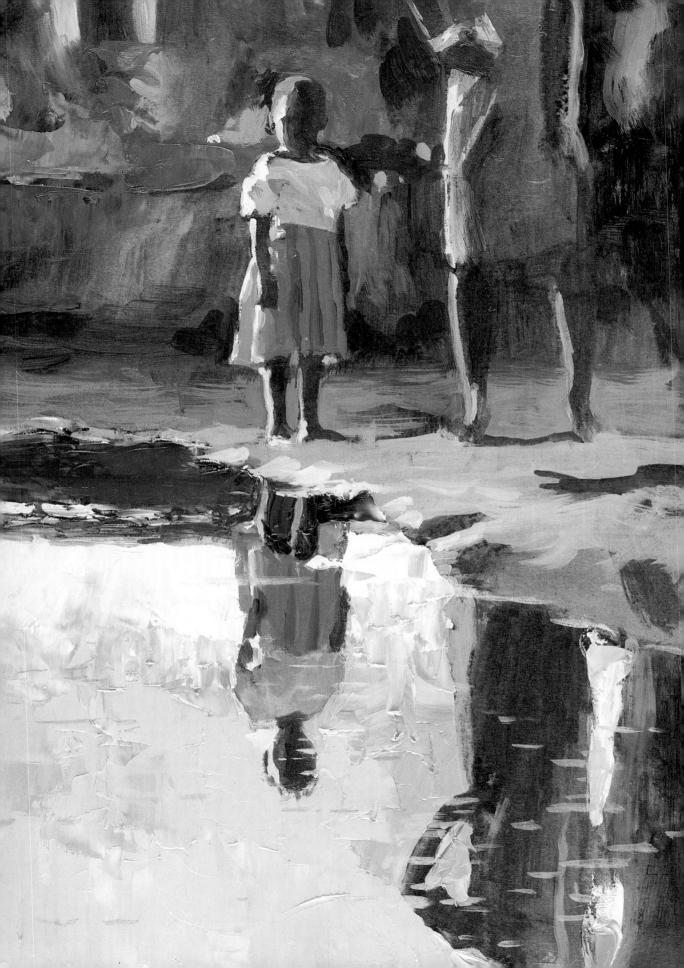

chapter 15

FURTHER AFIELD

Nowadays many people take vacations not for relaxation and leisure but to experience other cultures and climates. Others are posted for their work to places beyond their own background. In foreign and exotic locations it is easy to spot good subjects from among the unfamiliar surroundings. Where all is new and exciting we want to record it as best we can.

KEEPING A JOURNAL

An excellent way to respond to what is around you is to keep a diary-cum-sketchbook that records both visual and conceptual stimuli. Travellers' sketchbooks bristle with interest on every page. To make life simple draw with the same implement you use for writing – a pencil, waterproof felt-tip pen or mapping pen. These are all perfect accompaniments to watercolour, which is the easiest medium to carry around on lengthy travels. Choose a convenient-sized sketchbook that will also take the written word without difficulty. Carry your water in a small sealed jar and keep everything in a lightweight bag.

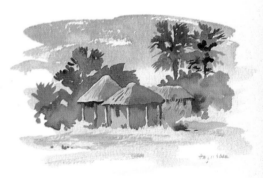

Into your book you can also paste tickets and stamps and visual memorabilia that represent landmarks of the journey and places you have visited.

> *... so difficult is it to be natural, so easy to be superior in our own opinion.*
>
> CONSTABLE

OPPOSITE: **Another World,** 30 x 20 cm (12 x 8 in), oil on board

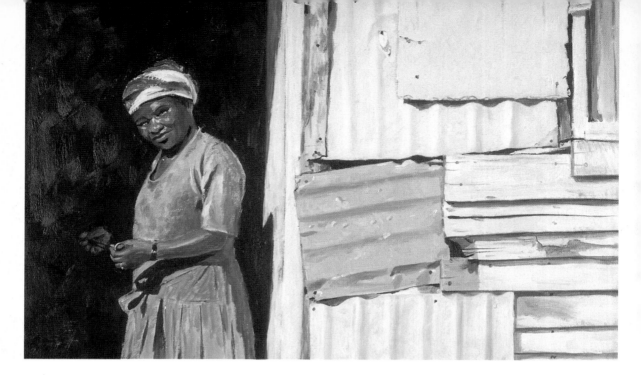

MUTUAL COURTESY

Always be aware that in some countries, especially in Africa, people may not like their photograph taken, and this may even extend to painting. Different cultures react differently to the artist in their midst. In Africa the children form a delightful crowd all around, leaving an arc of vision for the artist to see the subject. In India both adults and children are curious, and they crowd so close that it is often difficult to see the subject beyond the fray. In Spain the children are so helpful that they even ran across the road to ask the delightfully lounging tramp I was painting to sit up straight!

All these responses are such a privilege for the painter. There is little one can give in return, but bags of sweets never go amiss among the children and if someone specifically models for you, offer an appropriate payment for their help.

ROMANCING THE TONE

It is easy to romanticize that which is foreign to our daily life, and especially poverty. Shanty huts make delightful painting subjects with their quaint shapes, odd colours and myriad textures, but for those who reside in them living is hard and ablutions uncomfortable.

This does not mean we need feel guilty painting them, but we must be aware that what might be a happy subject for an afternoon's painting represents a very different lifestyle to someone else. Hopefully this awareness will transpose itself into the painting and make the image more poignant.

Chez Elsie

38 x 56 cm (15 x 22 in), oil on board
Elsie became a dear friend and invited me to her home. The corrugated sheeting of her walls were fascinating to paint; if you cover up the doorway they make an interesting image on their own.

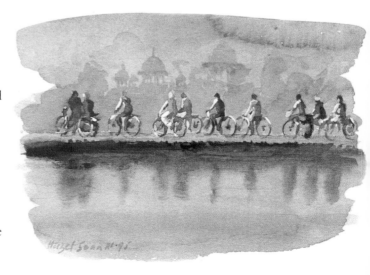

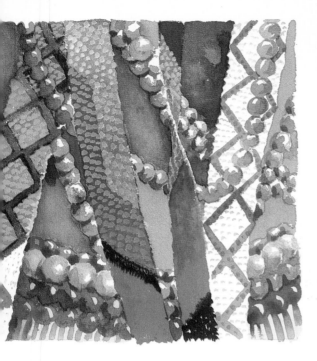

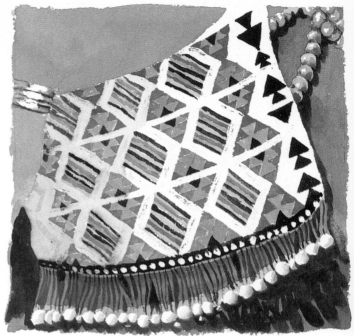

Zulu Beads

20 x 20 cm (8 x 8 in), watercolour
I was totally entranced by the
colours and patterns of the beads.
I zoomed in really close to
concentrate on them alone.

OPPOSITE: **Rush Hour, Agra**

10 x 15 cm (4 x 6 in), watercolour
Watching the endless stream of
bicycles cross the river bridge near
the Taj Mahal I could not resist
making a little painting. I washed
a blue-grey tint over all the paper,
bar the cyclists, to establish the
morning mood.

THE MICROCOSM

Aside from the amazing landscapes, unusual lifestyles and colourful costumes, look at the minutiae of the landscape, the little details that also make up the ambience of a place. The simple can be just as inspiring as the obviously exotic. Remember to zoom in and out of any view. The earthenware pots, hunky beads and local foods are the still-life staples of these other lands. The timeless nature of some of these items can be captured in even a quick study.

COLOUR AND CHARACTER

Never paint what you feel is required or expected of you, only what really interests you. Enough people have made a record, and your contribution is unique only if you bring something to your painting that is peculiarly your own.

Painting is not the same as depicting, just as writing is not the same as describing. Everybody will tell a different story about a visit to the same place.

If colour is your inspiration you will find it in abundance. Colourful dyes are one of the attractions of the African and Asian continents. Women in immaculately clean saris wash their clothes in the muddy waters of a river. African girls decked in patterned sarongs elegantly carry baskets upon their heads. The dashes of bright colour enliven any view, and when doubled by reflection in water they provide a field day for painters.

Find poses that say something specific about the men, women and children of the place. Faces alone can tell a tale, whether in the large languid eyes of the infant or the folded skin of the elder. If you are only passing through be aware that your responses are based on immediate impressions only. They may not represent the reality, but that does not lessen their validity or purpose.

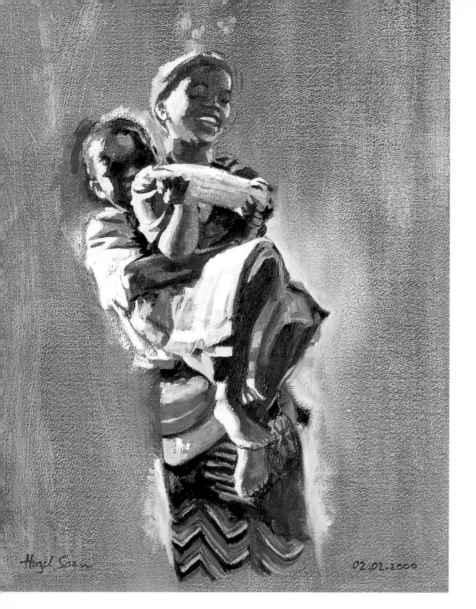

The Maize is Ripe

73 x 53 cm (29 x 21 in), oil on paper
Everything about this painting is upbeat: the pose, the smile, the warm background colour and the bright colours of the sarong. The whole painting is a celebration.

BELOW: **Penguins**

25 x 30 cm (10 x 12 in), watercolour
For these sketches I used Indigo, Sepia and Yellow Ochre, and a size 5 sable brush. I painted the bodies of the penguins in shapes, without line, looking up and down constantly to check what they looked like and where the brush was going.

PAINTING THE INTANGIBLE

There are also many intangible subjects to paint, such as community, tenderness, sadness, dignity. First, we must feel whatever we want to portray, then find the physical subject we think represents that emotion or concept. Next, we need to choose the appropriate medium and use colour and tone to good effect. Bright, warm colours denote cheerfulness and positive mood, while cool, blue, muted and dark colours can signify sorrow, hardship and negativity.

OUT WILD

To go into wilderness areas beyond the habitation of man is an invitation to endless inspiration. There is plenty to

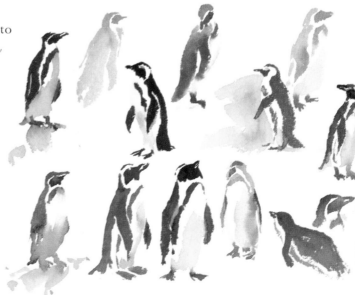

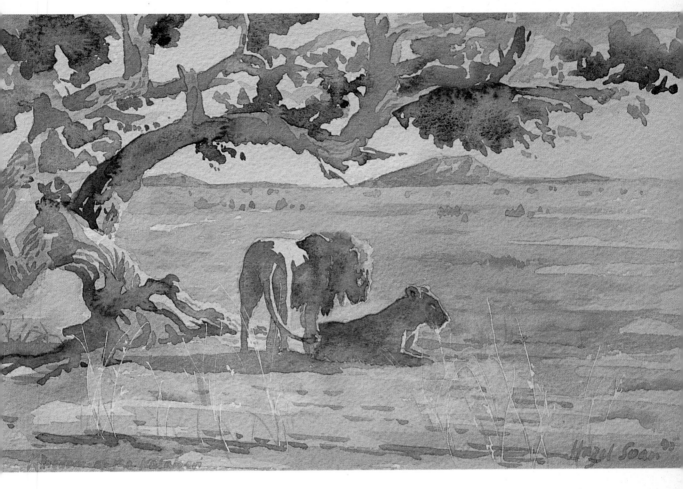

The Kingdom of the Kalahari

20 x 25 cm (8 x 10 in), watercolour
*The dry heat of the thirsty desert
setting is created with an overall
wash of Yellow Ochre and similar
but stronger colours painted on top
for the lions.*

Curiosity

18 x 13 cm (7 x 5 in), watercolour
*The stance of an animal is more
important than surface accuracy
and active brushmarks more
descriptive than careful detail.*

paint in this kind of environment, although some of it moves too
fast for the brush to record!

Just sitting, watching and listening, to absorb the ambience, is
the best way to begin. If you are painting animals watch with a
pencil in hand. Keep your eyes on the animal and draw its moving
shape over and over on the paper. Once you feel more familiar
with its lines, you are ready to work with a brush and to paint in
the shapes of the bodily form. Work in monochrome before
entertaining the thought of colour. Lively sketches can be
made in this way, which you can use in later compositions,
or enjoy just for themselves.

BACKGROUNDS AND SETTINGS

Setting your wildlife in a background is not always
necessary. If you are painting in great detail the
composition needs to be planned before you start
to paint. But if you just want to evoke an
environment you will find that loosely
washed backgrounds are sufficient. To
give the painting a warm atmosphere wash

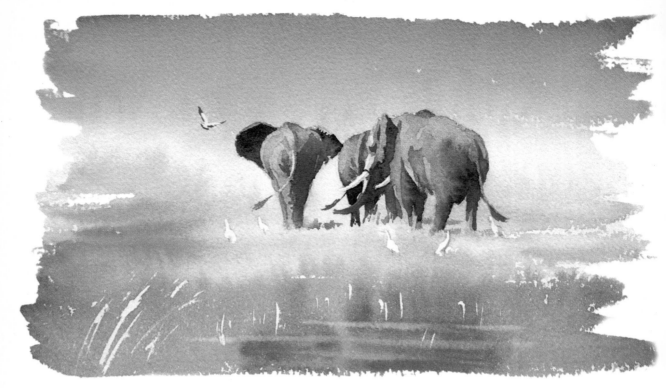

a pale Yellow Ochre or Burnt Sienna over the paper before painting on top. If you want to retain lighter highlights they can be left out of this wash or lifted out from this wash while it is wet.

FINISHED PAINTINGS

To make large compositions in the wild is difficult. In most places proximity to wild animals is dangerous and you must either stay in your vehicle or campsite or work in the protection of a hide.

The camera is therefore invaluable for the information you cannot record in paint. When transcribing from photographic reference in the shelter of your studio try to take yourself back into the wild, so that the fleeting movement is not stiffened. I used to have a refrigerator that whirred like the sound of cicadas in the bush: painting in its proximity sent me straight back on safari!

EXPOSURE TO THE ELEMENTS

You have seen how the effects of time and weathering offer exciting opportunities to the painter. In the wild the bleaching of bones, the weathering of dead wood and the cracking of earth are all interesting subjects in themselves and can also be transferred into paintings to provide authentic settings or focal points.

Desert landscapes long ravaged by lack of rain come in the most splendid colours of red and orange, ochres and purples. If you need a focal point to carry the eye into this cauldron of colour, look for a tree stump, tyre tracks or a lone animal. Even a few blades of grass breaking the horizon line can be enough to energize a mainly horizontal composition. Never over complicate your painting because you feel you have not done enough. Remember: 'most said with minimum means'.

Lake Kariba

*18 x 28 cm (7 x 11 in), watercolour
The majesty of African elephants moving through the bush needs little in the way of background. The blended washes of watercolour evoke the setting and leave us to imagine the journey off into the vast African expanse.*

Charge

*102 x 76 cm (40 x 30 in),
acrylic on canvas*
*Painting in the studio gives you
time to plan colour and
composition. In this painting the
wrinkled skin of the oncoming
rhino was the main interest, so all
my efforts were concentrated on the
colours and textures in quite a
stylized way.*

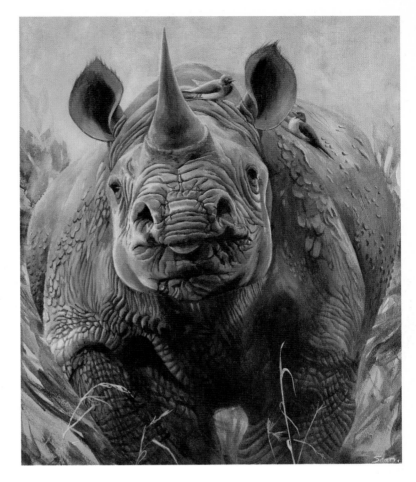

Road to Nowhere

20 x 28 cm (8 x 11 in), watercolour
*If, as I do, you like simple
landscapes and avoid green, the
desolate expanses of desert will
thrill you. The air is sometimes so
clear, as seen in this painting, that
the tones remain as strong in the
middle distance as they are in the
foreground.*

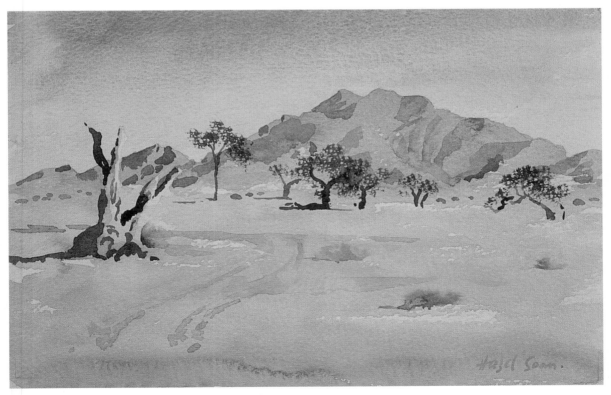

demonstration in watercolour
TO THE RIVER

COLOURS
Prussian Blue
Alizarin Crimson
Yellow Ochre

Painting on the hoof, so to speak, requires minimum equipment and time. When I am in the bush I carry very few colours. Any combination of blue, red and yellow will give you a satisfactory range for most natural subjects (see the colours I have chosen). This painting was made in the studio from photographs to show you how it is built up, but the process would be similar in the wild.

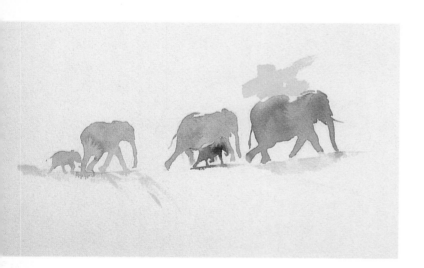

1 The herd of elephants is moving across the road. There is no time for a preliminary drawing, so the shapes of the elephants are painted straight onto the paper with a loaded brush in a tone equivalent to the light areas of their bodies. As one elephant moves on another will follow in a similar pose, so each painted elephant is likely to be made up of a number of real elephants!

2 The road is now empty, and the elephants have gone down to the river, so the background is washed in with soft wet-in-wet washes of Prussian Blue and Yellow Ochre. Directional brushstrokes are used for the road to indicate the rutted texture. The shadows of the bush across the road are merged with the greenery.

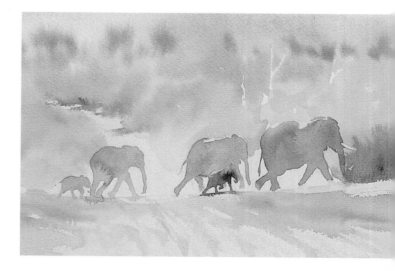

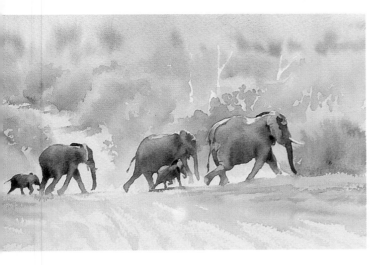

3 In real life I would try to move to where the elephants were drinking to paint the forms of their bodies, or wait for them to cross back over the road after their refreshment. But, using photographic reference, I carry on by darkening under the bellies and behind the ears to create their bulk. All three colours are used in varying proportions to make rich dark colours and kept wet to allow merging across the body form.

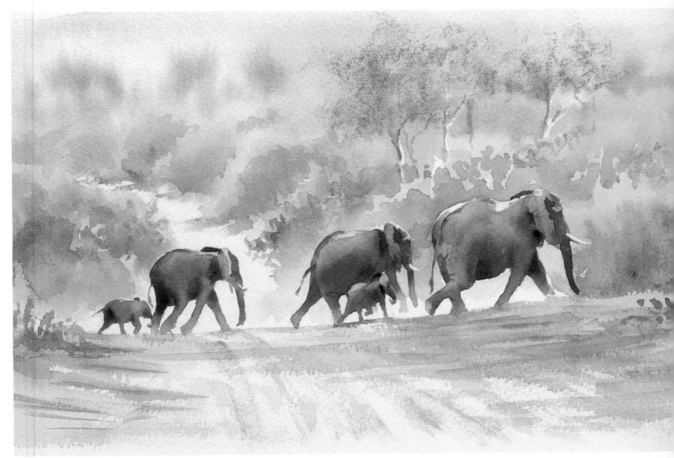

4 The foliage of some distant trees is sponged in with a small natural sponge. The foreground is too light, so a stronger shadow is cast across the foreground and the ragged verges are emphasized with stronger ochre and green. A touch of Alizarin Crimson into the background foliage ties the elephants and their surroundings together colourwise, creating a natural harmony in the landscape.

ABOVE: **To the River,** *25 x 41 cm (10 x 16 in), watercolour on 300 lb paper*

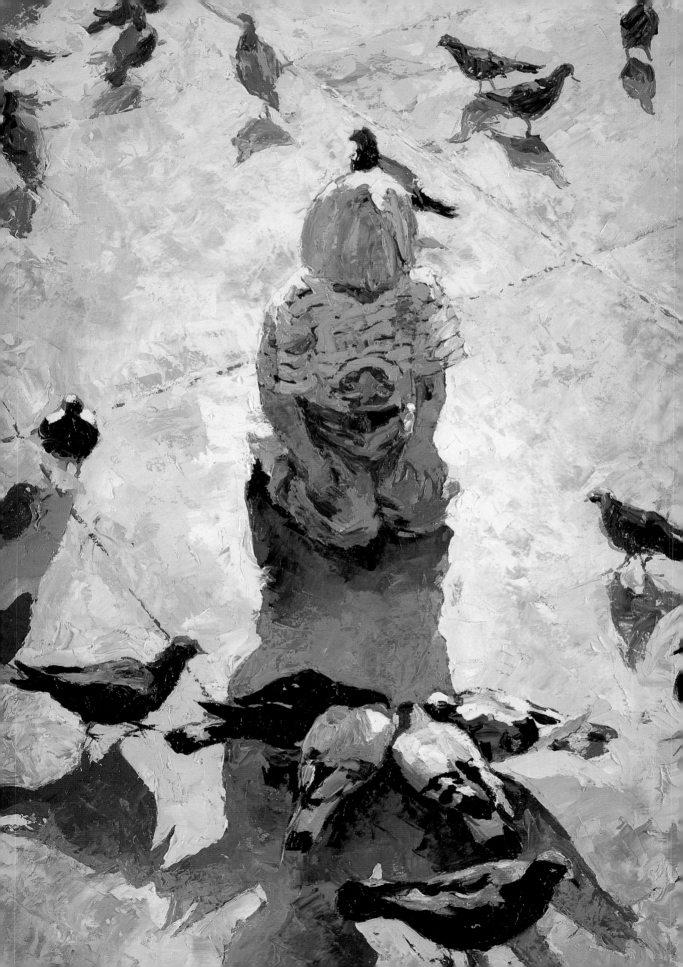

chapter 16

FROM THE HEART

The best paintings come into being through involvement.
The greater your interest in the subject the more likely
you are to enjoy the unfolding of the image on the surface
of the painting. If you are not excited by your subject
there is no point in painting it. I believe love of the
subject, love of painting, love of life itself, translates
directly onto the painted surface.

ZEAL FOR THE SUBJECT

The art of painting can express the intangible. Using
composition, colours and tones that emphasize emotions
the painter can evoke in the beholder a similar sentiment.
Before any subject abandon yourself to your first
impression. If you are really moved your painting will
convey to others the sincerity of your feelings.

Even if you have mastered technique and are competent
with the brush a painting that lacks enthusiasm will be
sterile. This is good news, because it means your fervour
is more important to the painting process than technique.
It means that at any point in learning to paint you can
make something worthwhile. This should give you
courage. It will help prevent you overworking a painting,
when in fact your statement is already valid.

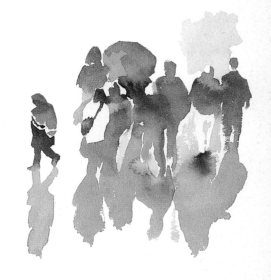

Reality is one part of art; feeling completes it ...

COROT

OPPOSITE: **Feeding the Five Thousand,** *56 x 41 cm (22 x 16 in), oil on paper*

IMAGINATION

For me visual inspiration comes from the physical world and the spirit it depicts. The enjoyment I experience from painting is the pleasure of seeing and translating what I see into paint. I do not really enjoy working solely from my imagination.

Some people, however, love to absorb what they see and paint from their memory later. If you prefer to do this, bear in mind the prerequisites of the painted surface and use composition, form, tone and colour to create the painting. If the information is not physically in front of your eyes you have ultimate control over your subject together with total responsibility.

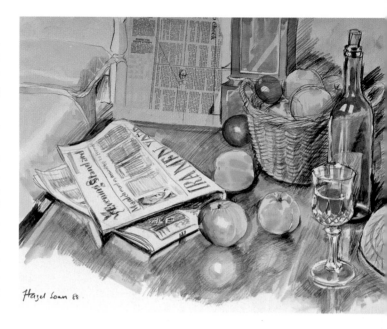

VISUAL MEMORY

A good visual memory for shape is a wonderful asset; to be able to sketch from life and then to remember those shapes at a later date without reference is a gift. But if you have this ability, when looking at a familiar subject, forget what you know and observe the site or object as if you have come upon it for the first time. When someone says to me, 'I know how to draw horses', I am instantly on

Peaches and Politics

*56 x 76 cm (22 x 30 in),
watercolour, conté crayon and
newspaper*
*Paintings have the power to
convey far more than the surface
subject matter.*

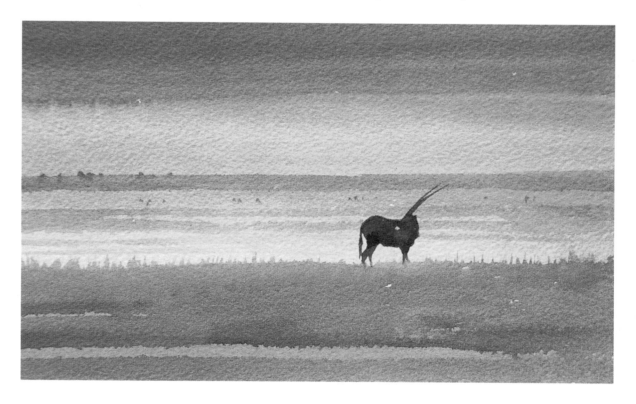

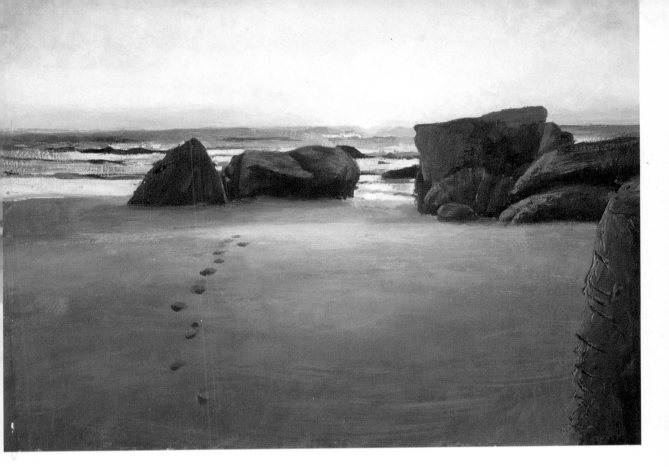

Hiding Place

25 x 30 cm (10 x 12 in), oil on board
A child saw his parents admiring
this painting in my studio. He told
his mother he liked the painting,
but please would she not buy it as
she would always be worried where
he was: the footprints went out to
the rocks, but did not come back.
Paintings speak louder than words.

OPPOSITE: **Standing Alone**
13 x 20 cm (5 x 8 in), watercolour
I have watched and painted many
oryx and yet each time I feel as if
this were the first. The shape of
each animal is unique and I really
enjoy the looking.

guard. A formula for making horses look like horses will impress, but not inspire. Use your asset if you have it, but remember to refresh it continually.

INSPIRATION AD INFINITUM

In an organized art class you might be asked to paint things that would not be your automatic choice, but if you have trained your eye to see shape, line, colour and tone and to delight in these elements instead of the subject per se, you will find very little that is not interesting to paint.

Once you start to look at any subject with a view to making a painting, the problems and opportunities are all the same: the needs of the two-dimensional picture plane, composition, colour, tone and texture.

If you cannot find these elements in the wider view, narrow your field of vision until you reach the simplest details of life. Somewhere there is something that interests you or you would never have picked up a paintbrush in the first place. There is no subject too humble, no subject too daunting.

As you get to know yourself and the subjects that you enjoy as a painter these catalysts will become more and more apparent. Practise painting whenever and wherever you can. Soon you will be crying, 'Stop! Enough! There's not enough time in the day to paint all the exciting things around me.'

Now you know how I feel about painting! You will never be at a loss for a subject again.

INDEX

Page numbers in **bold**
refer to illustrations